Nelson's
Youth Minister's
Manual

Nelson's Youth Minister's Manual

Theresa Plemmons Reiter

THOMAS NELSON
Since 1798

NASHVILLE   DALLAS   MEXICO CITY   RIO DE JANEIRO

© 2011 by Thomas Nelson, Inc.

Published in Nashville, Tennessee, by Thomas Nelson. Thomas Nelson is a trademark of Thomas Nelson, Inc.

Book design and composition by Upper Case Textual Services, Lawrence, Massachusetts.

Thomas Nelson, Inc., titles may be purchased in bulk for educational, business, fund-raising, or sales promotional use. For information, please e-mail SpecialMarkets@ThomasNelson.com.

Library of Congress Cataloging-in-Publication Data

ISBN-10: 1-4185-4502-3
ISBN-13: 978-1-4185-4502-4

Printed in the United States of America
1 2 3 4 5 6 QG 14 13 12 11

Contents

Introduction

I grew up in Western North Carolina, which is famous for beautiful mountains, friendly people, and good food. I can relate to all three. I love the Blue Ridge Mountains. My family is very friendly, and my mom and grandmothers were amazing cooks. I love to cook and learned all about cooking from my mother.

Learning to cook in the South is not always easy because many southern cooks do not use measuring utensils. Instead they just know how something should feel, what the texture should be, and what the consistency should be. Like other southern cooks, my mom did not measure with a measuring cup or spoon of any kind. She just "knew" exactly how much of each ingredient the recipe required.

Before my mom died, her church published a cookbook, and she submitted many recipes. I use my mother's recipes in that cookbook a lot, but I always laugh at the amounts listed for each ingredient because I know they truly are just estimates. I know my mother had to guess at what an exact measurement would be. Sometimes the dishes turn out well, but sometimes they do not. It is especially difficult to bake without using precise measuring.

Throughout my twenty plus years in youth ministry I have often thought that it would be great to have a "cookbook" to give me the recipe for success. To create a recipe for success in ministry would be impossible, right? After all, the ingredients and measurements would be different at each church. You cannot use a recipe with people, or can you?

I have written this manual to be your recipe for success. Whether this is your first year in ministry and you want to start out with the knowledge of a veteran, or you have been in ministry for years and feel your recipe is not working, this manual is for you.

This manual offers large amounts of experience mixed with faith, wisdom, and a dash of humor. My prayer is that you read this manual, and like a good southern cook, come up with the measurements that work for you.

Blessings,
Theresa Plemmons Reiter

Chapter 1

Trying Not to Give 511, So YGTP. This Stuff Is GTK.*
Understanding Youth Trends, Cultures, and Development Stages

Youth Trends and Cultures

Social Media

If you are entering youth ministry or have been in youth ministry over the past five years, you know how much of an impact social media has made on youth today. Youth feel they must be accessible to their friends at all times. Even the definition of the word *friend* has changed. Aristotle defined friendship as "a single soul, dwelling in two bodies." I have to tell you I have many friends on a certain social networking site and I really know nothing about their souls, but I consider them "friends." Friends used to be soul mates, but now they are a number that helps upgrade your status, or that of a person you know. It does not even have to be a person you know, like, or even trust. Youth actually communicate

---

*Trying Not to Give Too Much Information, So You Get the Point. This Stuff Is Good to Know.

with more people now than in any other time in history, but lack the ability to have verbal conversations and form intimate relationships. This is important for a youth minister to know because social media does make it easier to communicate with youth, announce upcoming events, and share daily Scriptures and prayer concerns. It does make it difficult, however, to teach youth to see Jesus as a friend. It can also be a challenge for youth to understand what it means to have a relationship with Christ. The words *friendship* and *relationship* are diluted.

Helpful Hint

Youth ministry must offer face-to-face interaction between volunteers and youth, as well as among the youths themselves.

Youth ministers today should use social media, but should realize the real, live interaction between youth and leaders is more important than ever. Youth need to see authentic love and compassion. Adult volunteers must be willing to talk and listen to youth through real conversations while looking them in the eyes. This type of relationship is rare. Youth ministry should also offer the avenue for youth to discuss topics face-to-face. I was recently in a meeting where a woman said her church was tired of fighting the cell phone battle, so they allow youth to read text messages in Sunday school classes and Bible studies. She said the youth needed to be available for their friends, and that she thought this policy was okay because she texted the students the Scripture of the day. I wanted to scream at the top of my lungs, *"What?"* The Bible does not say I will look to my mobile device for help or strength. It says:

> I will lift up my eyes to the hills—
> > From whence comes my help?
> My help comes from the LORD,
> > Who made heaven and earth. (Ps. 121:1–2)

Yes, you can ask youth to turn off and put away their mobile devices in order to spend time with God. You read it here. It really is *okay*! I have found youth actually feel relieved when they have some time away from texts and e-mails. Concentrate on helping them build real friendships with their peers and relationships with adults. Help them learn the art of verbal conversation.

Video and Electronic Games and the Making and Viewing of Videos

Video and electronic games are extremely popular among youth. I know very few teens who do not own at least one video gaming system. There is actually a business called Games2U that bring a bus-like truck to your house, church, or school. It offers all types of video games for children and youth. David Pikoff, the local franchise owner of the Games2U in my area, brings his games to many events on our campus. I will tell you Games2U is always the most popular activity at these events.

The majority of gaming enthusiasts used to be male, but females are quickly gaining in the statistics. The most popular games are ones where youth can create an avatar (graphic representation of themselves and/or friends). Youth enjoy being someone else, the hero, the talented dancer, or the professional athlete. Gaming not only provides entertainment, but a chance to escape reality. Gaming can become problematic when a teen loses contact with reality and cannot form real friendships. It is also important to know many games offer the opportunity to play online and youth can be playing and forming friendships with strangers who may or may not be their age.

The Entertainment Software Rating Board (ESRB; www.esrb.org/ratings/ratings_guide.jsp) rates video games for all of North America. The ratings are as follows:

- EC (Early Childhood, 3+): EC games contain no graphic images for violence.

- E (Everyone, 6+): E video games might have very mild language or violence.
- E10+ (Everyone, 10 and older): E10+ means the game could have mild violence and language, as well as some suggestive themes.
- T (Teen, 13+): T games contain violence, blood, swearing, and suggestive sexual themes.
- M (Mature, 17+): M games contain strong violence, language, sex, and blood.
- AO (Adults Only, 18+): AO games contain nudity, sexual content, or extreme violence.

Video games are a great way to get youth through the church door. These games can also be a great outreach. If you would like information on Christian video games you can go to inspiredmedia.com, or christiangaming .com. I would suggest you not only read reviews but you should also preview all games (both the Christian and non-Christian games) before you decide to use them in your ministry.

Money Matters

If I had written this book two years ago, the content would be entirely different when it comes to youth and money. According to Moneywatch.com teens today are more aware of the cost of clothes, games, and entertainment. The same youth who once felt a sense of entitlement for everything from watching television shows such as *Real Housewives of New York City, Atlanta,* or *New Jersey,* or *My Super Sweet Sixteen* now have a whole new view of money. According to moneywatch.com:

- 64 percent of teens are grateful for what they have.
- 58 percent are less likely to ask for something they want.
- 56 percent have a greater appreciation for hard work.
- 39 percent appreciate their families more.
- 73 percent believe in having an emergency fund.
- 51 percent understand debt.[1]

This is important for you as a youth director to understand because youth do not need or want extravagant programs or trips. They are more aware of the cost of ministry. It is great to include youth in planning your budget for every event. This helps them have a better understanding of money in general, and it especially helps them understand church budgeting. Youth who understand church budgeting and observe you setting a good example by being responsible with the church's resources are more likely to tithe now and in the future.

Developmental Stages of Youth

Youth development or adolescent development is the process through which youth acquire the cognitive, social, and emotional skills and abilities required to navigate life. It would be wonderful to have a beautiful graph here showing exactly how youth should behave at each age, but that is not possible. This experience of development is different for every youth based on his or her socioeconomic class and influences. Youth ministers have a big job!

Youth are constantly changing. They are moving from childhood to adulthood. The transition is emotional. It is difficult to navigate all the changes emotionally, socially, spiritually, and mentally.

So Many Influences, Too Little Time

Youth are influenced by their family, friends, school, media, the church, and more. It is difficult to even keep track of who and what influences our teens. However, despite the difficulty, it is vitally important to do so. Communicate with youth often about who influences them and why. Don't just talk about the life of Jesus and the love of God. Let youth see you live the words. They are most influenced by what they see, not what they hear. Youth have a unique way of mirroring adult culture in

painful ways. They can be hurtful to parents, adult volunteers, and friends, but never notice that they have hurt
someone.

Helpful Hint

How your youth group sees you behave will
affect each member more than what they hear
you say.

Many teens are in battles with their families. This
does not mean their families are bad or dysfunctional.
This period of a person's life is usually a time filled with
power struggles and the establishment of boundaries.
Parents need support as much as teens do during this
time.

Youth are trying to define who they are. Most teens
believe they are going to define who they are during
their teen years. It is important to teach youth that defin-
ing who you are is a journey, and this is the beginning.
Helping teens understand that life is a journey can help
take the pressure off them while still allowing them the
opportunity to learn that decisions they make now can
have a large impact on their future. Help youth see who
they are in Christ's eyes. There is no better time in a

person's life to read and understand the life of Jesus than his or her teen years. If we want to define who we are and who we are called to be, I truly believe it all begins with Jesus.

Youth in a Microwave

It seems that youth live in a microwave. They want immediate results. My family lives near many large theme parks. We have taken our son to one particular theme park countless times. We are fortunate to have a friend who works for one of the parks and knows how to navigate the park and avoid long lines. As a result, my son became accustomed to not having to wait in lines. When we visited another park he was quite frustrated when he learned he had to wait in lines like everyone else. He was used to immediate results, and he had to practice a lot of patience that day. Youth in general are not a patient group and really do not have a strong desire to learn patience. At my church we recently taught a Bible study on the fruit of the spirit. The fruit of the spirit most participants said they needed to work on was patience, but when we asked which one they were going to work on for the week, no one mentioned patience. They all said love or joy. I have to admit love and joy are much easier to practice than patience, and those two usually yield immediate results.

The "Down" Comforter

Many youth today have a sense of hopelessness and doom. They have lost their faith in politicians, teachers, church leaders, and other authority figures. This is not surprising if you watch the news. I believe youth do not want to feel this way. They are seeking strong leaders who truly live what they teach or preach. They want to be noticed, heard, and led.

I heard a story once that when someone asked June Carter Cash (a gospel and country music singer) how she was doing, she would answer "I am just trying to matter."[2] Many youth today are just trying to matter. They do not want to be hopeless. This is the time to teach them to put their faith in God, not people. Help them understand how the Holy Spirit is there to guide and comfort them. Guidance and comfort are two things every teen is seeking.

You are called to youth ministry, so put on your superhero cape. Take those ever-changing, easily influenced, dysfunctional, microwaveable, hopeless teens and introduce them to Jesus!

You have the power of God, the love of Christ, and the guidance of the Holy Spirit. You are well equipped!

Notes

1. Dan Kadlec, "Kids and Money: How Teen Attitudes Are Shifting," May 25, 2001, http://moneywatch.bnet.com/retirement-planning/blog/bank-dad/kids-and-money-how-teen-attitudes-are-shifting/1147/.

2. Hazel Smith, "Hot Dish: John Carter Cash Honors His Mama,"CMT, June 9, 2007, http://www.cmt.com/news/hot-dish/1564223/hot-dish-john-carter-cash-honors-his-mama.jhtml.

Chapter 2

Arrivals and Departures

I am not a fan of airports, with two exceptions: those in Charlotte, North Carolina, and Orlando, Florida. I love the airport in Charlotte because it has rocking chairs. Right there in the middle of the airport is a little piece of southern hospitality. Being from North Carolina, I have to love that. I can sit there between flights and just watch people come and go. There is a lot of entertainment offered right there in front of the food court. People are trying to watch their luggage at all times while juggling a tray of food. It takes a lot of coordination to travel these days. Gone are the good old days of "Would you mind watching my bag while I grab a Cinnabon?" No, you must carry everything with you up to the counter and haul it back to a table. Of course the only table available is in the very back, so you must travel through the maze of people and chairs to get to your seat. By this time the rocking chairs are all taken.

The Orlando airport is completely different. This airport is a very exciting place. It is usually filled with families traveling with children mixed in with the typical business travelers. It is an unusual mix that, of course, offers a great opportunity to people watch. The business travelers are on their laptops or phones being very careful not to look up for even a second. I truly believe they think if they look up some frazzled parent is going to hand them a screaming child and say, "Can you watch him for just a second while I go find my other three children?" You would be surprised how often that happens. They have learned. They never look up. Although it is quite fun to watch, it actually is not what makes the Orlando airport so intriguing to me; instead, it is the huge arrival and departure sign visible as one enters the terminal.

There you are, riding the escalator, and as you reach the top, there it is. It is the largest sign I have ever seen, and it lists all the arrivals and departures for the entire airport. There are chairs stationed all around it, so you can just sit and watch. The great thing about this sign is it is constantly changing. It just amazes me. It gives me a small glimpse of how many people are traveling the same day as I am and shows me how many places one can go on any given day. The opportunities are endless. Two things happen when I see this sign. The first is that I question my destination; I came excited about where I was going, but when I see the sign and think about where I *could* be going it takes away my excitement. It always seems like there are better destinations. Did I make the right choice? The second is that I wonder if pastors ever look at the arrival and departure signs in airports and think about their youth ministers. It seems they are always arriving and departing. I have always heard the average youth minister stays at a church for two years. I have actually never heard where this statistic came from, but I can tell you from being in youth ministry for more than twenty years and knowing many pastors that the statistic may be right on target. (I have not performed any type of statistical analysis on this subject because I have ADHD and would totally lose interest in the middle of the project.) I just know from what I observe on a daily basis.

It may seem silly that an entire chapter is devoted to arrivals and departures, but this may be the second most important chapter in the book behind the one on child protection.

Arrivals

If you plan on arriving at any church, you must first get the job. If you plan on getting a job, you have to apply for a position. If you want to apply for a position, you have to know about the position for which you are applying. So, let's start at the beginning.

How do I find churches that are seeking youth ministers? There are many ways but here are the top four resources I have used to help search committees and youth ministers find the right fit for them.

1. Networking

   Ask friends, professors, and colleagues. Use social networking sites such as Facebook or Twitter. This works well if it is your first position or if you are not currently serving a church. No pastor wants to read on Facebook his or her youth minister is looking for another church. (Don't laugh. It has happened.) If you do not want your church to know you are considering other options, have friends from college or seminary post something about you and what you are looking for. Ask them not to be too specific and not to use your name. I found an amazing youth minister through Facebook for a friend of mine. He ended up being a friend of a friend and he was just what the church was looking for.

2. Youth Specialties (*www.youthspecialties.com*)

   This site has a wonderful job bank. You can search by denomination or region. You can also post your résumé. Check the site often. Remember that it takes an average of a year for most churches to fill a position, so do not just check current listings. This is a free search. Churches pay a fee to post job positions.

3. Church Staffing (*www.churchstaffing.com*)

It offers current job openings as well as tips for those looking for positions within the church.

4. Youth Ministry Architects (*www.ymarchitects .com*)

Job boards post listings of opportunities from all denominations.

The Application Process

I know you have been told to send a cover letter and résumé to the church or chairperson of the search committee, but I will tell you to call the church first and ask to speak directly to the pastor. I will not apply to a church unless I have spoken with the senior pastor.

I have learned that if the youth ministry job is really important to the pastor, he or she will take the time to speak with you. Keep the call brief. It is not an interview. Introduce yourself and give a quick overview of your qualifications and ask what he or she is looking for. A senior pastor is very busy, but if he or she is looking to fill a key position, he or she will speak to you. If he or she is not in, do not leave a message. Call back. He or she has a million messages to return each day, so ask when would be a good time to call back. Ask, "What are the strengths and weaknesses of the current youth ministry, and what characteristics would the ideal youth minister possess?" Listen carefully to the person's answers. If the senior pastor does not have a lot of knowledge of the youth ministry or is overly negative, it may indicate that this church is not a good place to serve. If you have a sense of humor, and he or she does not, it may prove to be a difficult working relationship, should you serve there. If the conversation is awkward, uncomfortable, or strained, chances are that is how your relationship will be if you are on staff. You want to work for a pastor(s) who is approachable.

I have had the honor of working with some of the most amazing pastors. They each have served as my pastor, supervisor, mentor, and friend. It all began with a telephone conversation.

Research

Find out as much as possible about the church. If the church has a Web site, check out the entire site. Do not just focus on the section dedicated to youth ministry. Also research the children's ministry. You need to know about the children's ministry even if you do not have children. The children's ministry plays a huge part in the success of the youth ministry. Both ministries will have a greater chance of success if the leaders of each work together. Look for the strengths in the children's ministry, and be prepared to build on them to have success in middle school ministry. If there is not much offered for children, be prepared to start from scratch with middle schoolers.

Cover Letter

Find out who you should send the letter and résumé to. Do not use "To Whom It May Concern." It should be addressed to a person.

Keep the letter brief. Introduce yourself, make a statement about the church, and say why you are interested in working there. You may include personal information if you wish, but it is not necessary. I found it important to say I was married with a son, and my husband could work from anywhere in the country. Churches cannot legally ask such things in the interview. I wanted them to know it was easy for me to change locations. If you are applying for a church associated with a different denomination than your experience will show, tell about how your theology is in line with the theology of the church in which you are applying.

Use a quality-stock paper or résumé paper for your cover letter and résumé. Use a common, easy-to-read font.

Résumé

The top of the résumé should say who you are and give all your contact information, including your e-mail address. If you have an e-mail address that begins with "bunny," "partygirl," "superdude," or "slackerstudent," you may want to consider opening a new e-mail account with a more appropriate title. Next, list your educational accomplishments. Do not include degrees unless you have them. If you are a student, you may want to include your field of study and a list of your ministry experience with the most recent position at the top. It is important to note which are volunteer positions as opposed to paid positions. Keep the résumé to one page if possible. I have had to sort through hundreds of résumés, and the ones that get my attention are precise, well written, and list the experience and education I am looking for. You may include a photo, but make it one that genuinely represents you. You do not want it be too serious or too playful. If you have to choose between the two, go with a professional photo, with you wearing a suit. You may be a great surfer, but a surfer photo will most likely not get you an interview.

The bottom of the résumé should say "References available upon request."

References

Should references be required they should be listed on a separate page because some churches will contact references before conducting interviews and before you have notified your current church that you are searching.

Make sure you ask everyone on your reference list for their permission to use you as a reference. You should include people who are not related to you, have known you for at least three years, have observed you in ministry, can vouch for your character, and can provide adjectives to describe you and your ministry style. You should include a professor (if you are a current student or recent graduate), a pastor, and a volunteer who has worked with you in ministry. Be careful about choosing friends as references. I once was hiring a student who was currently in college to work as an intern. When I asked the applicant's friend for adjectives to describe her friend she said "cool" and "nice." I did not find the reference to be particularly helpful.

Now to the fun stuff!

The Interview

You can learn a lot about a church before you meet one single person from the church, especially if you will travel to the interview from out of town. If the church has a difficult time making your travel arrangements and relaying information to you, it most likely has a difficult time communicating with its staff. If you are given contradicting information from several people, that is a red flag. I once spoke to four different people regarding my travel arrangements. I arrived at the airport and waited for more than an hour for someone to meet me. When the person from the church arrived, he spent twenty minutes telling me how busy he was without apologizing for my loss of time. The entire interview felt chaotic. This is a red flag, my friend, and when it occurs you should run like the wind.

A Memorable Interview

My most memorable interview was at Hyde Park United Methodist Church in Tampa, Florida. I had already planned an adult mission trip to the east coast of Florida to provide hurricane repair and cleanup. I planned for a friend in Titusville to take me to Tampa at the end of the week for my interview, and I would fly home. The team would leave me with friends in Titusville and drive back to Spartanburg, South Carolina, where I was then serving.

When we arrived in Florida we were able to work one day in Titusville when we received word that another hurricane was headed to the east coast. We left Titusville and headed to Orlando. We worked one day in Orlando and were told we needed to leave because the storm was headed inland. I called Hyde Park United Methodist Church and told them our mission team had to head west and we were in need of a place to stay and we were willing to provide assistance in any way possible.

The staff worked together to provide us with everything we could possibly need for our stay. Members had dropped off sleeping bags, pillows, and blankets, and the young adult minister had arranged for us to work at a food distribution warehouse.

It was a wonderful experience, but after one day the hurricane was now headed to the west coast, and the mission team had to head home. That left me with the decision to ride back to South Carolina with my mission team or stay in Tampa for my interview that was now three days away. I spoke with the associate pastor, and the church offered to check me into the hotel early and cover the extra expenses, so

I could stay for the interview. The hurricane seemed to be losing strength, and we felt it was safe for me to stay. It was my first hurricane and I rode it out on the fourth floor of a hotel in downtown Tampa. After about six hours, the hotel lost power, and water started pouring into my room from around the window. It soaked the entire briefcase of items I had brought for the interview. Since there was no power, the vending machines did not work, and the restaurant in the hotel closed. There I was with no food. The hotel gave us bottled water, and I was able to find one Rice Krispies treat given to me by one of the youth on the trip.

Thirty-two hours later the storm blew over, electricity returned, and I was able to meet the program staff from Hyde Park United Methodist Church for breakfast at a nearby restaurant. I was very hungry. We all sat down for breakfast, and they began asking me questions. I looked at them and asked, "May I please eat first? I am starving!" They laughed and said, "Of course." They were kind and understanding. I knew I wanted to be a part of their staff even if it meant I had to live in a state where hurricanes happen. I served happily at Hyde

Park for several years and always felt honored to be a part of the congregation and staff. They were willing to go above and beyond to make my mission trip experience and interview experience go as smoothly as possible.

Not every church can make the interview process seem smooth through a hurricane, but Hyde Park did. I served there happily for several years and remain close to the staff and many members of the congregation. It was a privilege to serve there.

Before the Interview

When you have an on-site interview, ask for a job description and schedule of interviews/meetings, and so forth. If you are expected to lead a youth event or Bible study, be prepared!

During the Interview

- Dress professionally, but be comfortable. Interviews often end with a tour of the church. This is not the time for wearing new shoes.
- Be prepared. Make copies of your résumé for everyone. Do not assume the church will have copies.

- Write down names of everyone on the interview committee and try to call them by name. Make eye contact and avoid turning your back on someone while addressing a question.
- Smile and be yourself. It is okay to be nervous and it is okay to say you are nervous.

  I had been in ministry a long time and had been through many interviews, but when I met Jim Harnish, the pastor at Hyde Park, I could not complete a sentence. I had read all his books and was so excited to meet him that I forgot I was being interviewed. Thank God he has a sense of humor.

- If you have youth calendars, newspaper articles about previous youth groups, or articles you have had published, bring them.
- Have a list of questions prepared for the committee and for the youth. Do not ignore youth if they are included on the committee, but do not address just the youth.
- Do not ask about salary or benefits in the interview.
- If your current church does not know you are looking to move, ask the committee to not check references unless they are planning to

hire you. Talk to your pastor and adult leaders before they hear the news elsewhere.

- Go to jobinterviewquestions.org then click "Job Interview Questions," and then click "Illegal Interview Questions." You do not have to answer any questions that are illegal. If someone asks you a question that is illegal, just state you are not comfortable answering that question.

    I was once asked during a church interview, "Who does your laundry?" I replied with a simple question, "Have you asked this question of the male candidates who have interviewed for this position?" The pastor in the interview quickly apologized for the man who asked the question and ended the interview. I chose not to continue the interview process.

- Ask how long previous youth ministers have stayed. Ask why they left. If interviewers are negative and discuss personal matters about previous staff, that is a red flag.
- Ask the people on the committee why they joined the church and what they like about it.
- Ask how the community describes the church.
- What is the mission of the church?
- What is the mission of the youth group?

- Is there a group of adults in place who currently work with the youth? How were they chosen and trained?
- What is the youth ministry budget?

You Have Been Offered the Position

This is the time to discuss some very important issues before you accept the position.

- Salary: it is important to realize that some states do not have state income taxes, so the pay may seem higher or lower depending on this. Know the cost of living for the area in which you will be living.
- Insurance coverage: is it offered for your family?
- Pension
- Vacation and time away
- Continuing education: are you able to continue your education and does the church provide funding?
- Work hour expectations
- Does the church offer discounts for childcare or preschool?
- Ask for a copy of the personnel policies or church handbook before you accept the position.

- Ask for clarification about days off following youth trips, retreats, etc.
- Know who will be your immediate supervisor and if that is likely to change. (At one church I had three different supervisors in two years.) This is not uncommon.
- Ask to spend a few minutes with other staff members. Ask how long they have been at the church. Ask what they like and what they feel is most challenging. (Note: if the staff is overstressed, unfriendly, or unhappy, chances are if you work there, you will be unhappy too.)
- Ask if you may contact the previous youth minister. Ask him or her about his or her experience working at the church. Listen carefully. Do not assume you will be the exception to the rule.
- Ask if moving expenses are paid by the church, and, if so, how will they be paid. Make sure to pay for moving insurance.

Arrivals

How you arrive at a church can set the tone for your ministry for a very long time. It is important you know how to arrive. I have had good arrivals and bad arrivals.

Good Arrival: The youth have filled your entire office with balloons the night before and you have to burst each balloon with a pin before your office furniture arrives. It is bad for the offices that surround your office, but good for you because you know for sure the youth group is thoughtful and fun.

Bad Arrival: You are asked to put all your office books, supplies, and so forth across the hall from your office because there is someone currently occupying your office.

Good Arrival: You are told by the pastor to go home and get your house settled before you start work.

Bad Arrival: You are asked to clean up the messy office left by the previous youth minister.

Good Arrival: The youth leaders meet you at the door of your new home when you arrive with the moving truck. They have filled your refrigerator and cabinets with groceries and are there to help you unpack.

Bad Arrival: You take the youth leaders out to dinner at a fancy restaurant because you have a gift certificate and want to do something nice for them, and they think you are spending the entire youth budget on a fancy dinner. This was also bad communication on my part.

How to Make a Bad Entrance

Never say a bad word about the previous youth minister. This is especially difficult if everyone around you is saying negative comments. It is best to change the subject. If people complain about the previous youth program, ask them how they tried to change it for the better or what would be their suggestions for the future. Some people are just complainers, and others really want to help. Try to discern the two as early as possible. Stay away from church and staff gossip. Change the subject to a positive topic such as a lunch or the locations of the restrooms.

Do not ask for anything for your office the first week, if at all possible. If your chair is broken, try to use it for at least a week. Chances are, someone will ask you if you need anything and that will be your chance to ask if there is another chair for you to use. Do not assume the church will just buy a new chair. Once I simply asked for a new chair since my chair sat so low to the ground that I looked like a five-year-old behind the desk. Because of my request, I was told by a coworker that everyone thought I was demanding. Seriously, I should have just asked for phone books and sat on them. No one likes a demanding staff person. Also remember that all churches are different, and administrative duties are divided differently. I am horrible with computers and

I do not know anything about graphic design. I always ask before I accept a position if there is help available in that area or a budget designated for printing and design.

How to Make a Good Entrance

Speak to everyone on staff and learn names. Many churches use volunteers to answer the telephones. Do not assume they know your name and position. I had worked at a church for months when my husband called and asked to speak to me. He was told there was no one at the church with that name. He told them I was the youth minister. They politely told him the name of the previous youth minister and hung up. He called me on my cell phone and said, "You may want to go to the front desk and tell them who you are and that you work there." It took about two weeks for me to get to all the volunteers, but they finally knew my name and position. I also made some great friends. They were wonderful to work with.

Ask if you can move the furniture in your office. Try to make the office different from the previous youth minister's. This helps youth make the transition and see this as your space. If there are pictures of the current youth members in the office, do not remove them and replace them with the youth group you just left. You may miss those teens, but it will be hurtful to the new group. Find a fun and new way to display them. You may want to take pictures at your first youth event, so you can replace old photos with new photos.

Ask youth to help you unpack and decorate your office. This is a great way for them to get to know you and an easy way to start forming relationships. As they unpack pictures of your family or previous youth on a trip or retreat, ask the youths about their families or church trips they have enjoyed. Ask them about their schools and friends. They will have many questions for you, so be prepared. Be careful about asking youth to help you unpack at your home. Never invite a youth to your home without another adult present. Invite two or three youths to help at a time. Remember to keep your office door open if youth are present.

Meet with your adult leaders as soon as possible. Include Sunday school teachers, and Wednesday night and Sunday night leaders. Discuss the current youth schedule. It is important for you to have a clear understanding of all youth activities, studies, and so on. Get to know the leaders. It is important to ask if they are planning to keep their current positions. You should ask them to stay. Some volunteers believe they are done when the new youth minister is hired. Unless there is an urgent need for change, keep everyone in their current positions for at least three months. This is the minimum time needed to observe the current program. The first three months should be about forming and building relationships, not overhauling the ministry. It is too much to try to do both. Observe and work with the current leaders. Ask them to help you develop a long-range plan for ministry. If you plan to implement change, have key leaders on board and behind you. Do not assume what worked for your previous youth group will work at every church. I know many youth ministers who have a "one-size-fits-all" youth ministry. They try to apply this to every church. It simply does not work. You must know the people you are ministering to and the needs of the group. Build your ministry around the needs.

Give Youth an Opportunity to Grieve

Sometimes churches can be in a rush to hire someone for the youth ministry position without understanding the youth group may not be ready for a new person. This is especially the case when the previous youth minister has been there a long time. Youth and adults have formed strong bonds, and they are grieving the loss. It is important for them to have time to grieve. Let them express their feelings, and do not take them personally. Their love for the previous youth minister has little to do with you. Tell them you are sorry they miss their friend, and listen to stories of youth trips or ministry experiences. Give them time, and be patient with them.

Find Out Where the Sacred Cows Are

It is important to know what are traditions and expectations of the group. Know from the start what trips, retreats, camps, events, and so forth are important to the group.

I have learned this the hard way. I had been at a church for about three months when I called a meeting of the adult and youth leaders to discuss the summer mission trip. It was early January, so I thought we had plenty of time. The group informed me they had **always** participated in Appalachia Service Project (ASP), and they loved it. That was their only choice. I called the next day to find out the deadline for the application was in November, which happened to occur on my first day on the job. Needless to say we had certainly missed the deadline, and all weeks were full. I had no idea how to tell the youth group. I spent the next two weeks secretly trying to find a great alternative to ASP, so I would not disappoint the entire high school mission group. But, to my surprise, we received our mission assignment from ASP. It was scheduled for the usual week, and we could add or subtract up to five people. I was absolutely speechless. I called to find out when they had received the application, and they could not find it right away. They called back a few days later to say that the application from the previous year had ended up in the current file and they had made the assignment. They wanted to know if we could still come. I believe it was a miracle. It may not seem miraculous to you, but to a new youth minister it was miraculous! We had a wonderful mission trip, and it was not until years later that I shared the story with the youth and adult counselors. I have never missed a mission deadline since.

Departures

Many youth ministers ask me how I knew it was time to leave a church. There are many factors that play important roles in making the decision to leave a church. Sometimes you just know it is not the right fit. If you are unhappy going to work each day, and you do not enjoy serving with your ministry team, then pray for God to help you mend the current relationships or send you to a new church. Do not just assume you should leave a church because the work is hard and the hours are long. Ministry is not easy, and it cannot be done without prayer and leadership from God. Do not even think about leaving a church until you have spent time in prayer. If you are married, it is important to discuss your thoughts with your spouse. Pray together for God's guidance.

Here are some questions to ask yourself before you consider leaving your current position.

- Is my ministry here effective?
- Have I achieved the ministry goals I set?
- Is the ministry growing?
- Do I have effective adult leadership?
- Am I currently compensated enough to provide for my needs?
- Is the ministry centered on me?
- Have I given my all to make this ministry succeed?
- Have I equipped others to lead?
- Am I in constant conflict with the leadership or the theology of this church?
- Do I feel I could do better elsewhere?

There are several reasons youth ministers leave positions. The number one reason is burnout. At least youth ministers will say it is burnout. It should be called exhaustion. Youth ministry is like no other ministry in the church. It can completely consume you, and you will not even realize it. You may feel the need to leave just because you want to rest. You know the first three months at a new church is the honeymoon stage, and you long for that time. This does not mean you should leave. You may need to take a hard look at your schedule, and take some time off for prayer and discernment. Every year, I am ready to quit my job about two weeks before my vacation. I tell myself I want to be a stay-at-home mom.

I have told myself this for the last ten years. I have not quit because, while I am on vacation, I think about the previous year and what amazing things I have witnessed and the beautiful children I have the opportunity to minister to, and I am ready to come back and start it all over again. I learn each year to delegate more and fill in fewer squares of the calendar.

Many youth ministers leave after two years in a church because that is when the real work begins. The first year is about building relationships and observing. The second year is about developing a ministry plan. The third year is when the plan begins to take place, and that is hard work. It is also where the most important youth ministry begins. Do not leave just because the job gets difficult.

Reasons to Leave

If you ever feel that no one else can do your job, and the youth ministry at your church could not survive without you, it is time to leave. Read the sentence again.

It is important to realize the church was there before you, and it will be there when you leave. God is in control of that youth group. You are not. I know this is hard to read, but believe me it is true. I have been blessed with some amazing youth groups. I am not afraid of hard work, and I have given every church my all, but I have never believed for one minute that *I* did it. It was only by the grace of God and the leading of the Holy Spirit that anything was accomplished. Once your forget this, your ministry is over. It then becomes an ego trip.

I do believe you can be happily serving a church, and God will call you to another church. This does not necessarily happen by a telephone call, e-mail, or text, but it can. A friend of mine once told me about a youth ministry position at a church. I was not interested and passed the information on to friends in case they were interested. It was a great church, but I did not want to move. We lived close to my family, our son was happy, we loved our church, and we had great friends. The ministry was growing and going well. I tried to forget about the church, but I just could not get it out of my mind. I even prayed for God to take it out of my mind. I did not even want to think about moving. That is when I began thinking about it even more. The more I prayed, the more it stayed in my mind. Then I realized I was going to be in Florida on a mission trip and could easily go for an interview. Well, as you read at the beginning of this chapter, it was where God wanted me. I truly felt it.

The Departure

CHOOSING TO LEAVE. There are few things as important as how you depart a church. You must give the church as much notice as possible, but know it is very easy to check out of a position once you have accepted another. You must also give the church time to grieve and prepare for a new person. It should be at least two weeks, but one month is the standard. No youth minister worth beans would leave at the beginning of a summer. You can choose to be helpful or resentful. Helpful is always best. Do not be offended if your job is posted on a Web site before you leave the pastor's office. Good youth ministers are hard to find, and churches know finding one can be a lengthy process. The pastor and search committee have to do what is best for the church and the youth. Respect that over your own need to be recognized. All churches handle departures differently. You may receive a huge going away party at a church where you served as a summer intern and a going away card from a church you served for five years. I cannot tell you what is standard because churches do not know. It depends on the church, denomination, and the size of the church. Larger congregations experience many staff changes, so they may celebrate your ministry on a smaller scale. It is not a reflection of your ministry or a reflection of you. You are the one who chose to leave. (If it was not your decision, read the next paragraph.)

WHEN IT ISN'T YOUR CHOICE. The most difficult departure is when it is not your decision. There are usually many warning signs before a person is asked to leave a position. The first warning sign is an average or below-average evaluation. This can be a formal evaluation or a number of meetings with your pastor asking you to make changes. You may feel the changes do not need to be made or wait to make the changes. Trust me. That is a job evaluation and should be taken seriously.

If you are asked to leave for any reason it is important that you leave with grace. Do not try to build support or gather a following. Do not speak negatively about the church to the youth. Remember, the ministry has to go on, and youth do not need to be involved in a church political battle. You do not have to agree with the reasons, and you cannot control what people say about you. Place your trust in God. Learn from mistakes, and find a place to heal.

If you feel you should leave the ministry, seek the counsel and guidance of spiritual leaders you trust. Pray and trust God to lead you to a place to serve. You do not have to be in ministry to serve. God always has a place for those who love him and are willing to follow him.

Depart and serve!

Chapter 3

Rip Currents, Waves, and Sea Creatures
Avoiding the Hazards that Can Pull a Youth Minister Under

One of the benefits of living in Lakeland, Florida, is the ability to get to a number of beautiful beaches in a short amount of time. I love the beach. Our family heads to the coast every chance we get. The ocean is beautiful, but its beauty is misleading. It can appear calm and beautiful on the surface, but beneath that surface it can be dangerous. In 2005 the Florida legislature adopted a uniform flag system to provide beach safety. Flags flown in various colors indicate potential dangers to beachgoers.

The definition of each flag is as follows:

- Double Red Flags
  The beach is closed because it is too dangerous for swimming.

- Red Flag-High Hazard
  High surf and strong currents mean it is best to stay out of the water.

- Yellow Flag
Moderate surf means one should exercise caution.

- Green Flag
Low hazard risk makes the beach favorable for swimming and indicates calm conditions.

- Purple Flag
Dangerous marine life has been spotted. Marine pests are present.

I am embarrassed to admit that I had to look up the meaning of each color. As much as we go to the beach, I was not aware of the specific dangers and precautions we should take.

In youth ministry there are specific dangers, and the comparison to drowning is an accurate one. You can drown in your own ego, get into situations over your head, or get caught up in the strong currents of gossip, popularity, numbers, money, power, fads, and expectations. If only there were a universal system in place to provide ministry safety and sanity. It would be wonderful for youth ministers to know how to lead students to Christ while avoiding the dangers that can affect or stop their ministry. Since there is no universal flag system in place, use this chapter to help you navigate around the minefields and avoid pitfalls in youth ministry.

Double Red Flag: The Ego-Driven Ministry

When I interviewed for my current position, I was asked a question that caught me off guard. I must admit that with more than twenty years of church interview questions stockpiled in my head, I am rarely surprised by any question, but this one surprised me. The pastor asked me if I had an ego. I had never been asked that. Was it a trick question? I had to be honest so I said, "Yes, I do have an ego." He said, "Good." He thanked me for my honesty and said he could tell I had a healthy ego. In his experience, he has found that people with healthy egos strive for perfection. He wanted his ministry team to have egos. The key word in the conversation was *healthy*. There are several definitions of the word *ego*. The ego controls thought and behavior, and it is most in touch with one's external behavior. It can mean pride in one's self, self-esteem, or an exaggerated sense of self-importance.

In youth ministry, more than any other ministry area, one can have an exaggerated sense of self-importance. This is dangerous and is worthy of a double red flag. Close down the beaches! The ego has caused strong currents that can pull any youth group under!

Remember Your Place

Youth ministers are the center of attention and can easily develop a following. It is important to always keep

Christ as the center of your ministry and remember you are a vessel. You are not the most popular kid in the group. You are not the center of the universe. You are a person chosen to serve God in a mighty way. You should constantly be equipping leaders to help youth grow in their faith. I was taught that a good youth minister should always be working himself or herself out of a job. I believe that. I am constantly looking for strong leaders who are trained, loving, role models, and leaders. My greatest success in youth ministry has been when I have left churches, and the volunteer youth counselors kept the ministry going without skipping a beat. They have welcomed new youth ministers into the church with love, excitement, and true hospitality. To me that is the one definition of success. I knew the ministry was not about me. If I ever thought the youth program was about me, or that the church could not get along without me, I knew it was time to go. The church is in God's hands, not mine. God was in control before I got there, and would continue to be in control when I left.

My first interest in youth ministry came from watching my youth minister when I was a teen. I thought my first youth director was the coolest man in the world, and we got to play awesome games. Youth ministry is fun, no doubt about it. You get to play great games, travel to wonderful places, meet interesting people, eat a lot of junk food, and play a lot of games.

Games are important, and my director knew that, but he also was a great teacher and example. He was a college student at the time, and we were his first church. He was the first person to tell me you had to go to college to be a youth minister. I seriously had no idea why someone would have to go to college to lead games and teach Bible stories. I am sure glad he taught me that youth ministry was about much more than playing games.

Warning!

A little nugget of advice: if you are going into youth ministry because of the fun and games, please read chapter 10, "Life and Times of a Real Youth Minister."

Red Caution Flag: Money

It is important to always consider your accountability and how to avoid temptation when it comes to dealing with money. You should work to protect yourself as well as your volunteers. It is best to have responsible laypeople receive and count money for trips, events, and so forth. Here is a list of tips:

- Always have two people counting and recording all amounts. One person should never be alone while money is being counted or accepted.
- The money should be placed in an envelope and sealed.
- Two people should place their signatures over the sealed part of the envelope.
- People should always know where to place the money such as a lockbox, safe or designated drop area, or file cabinet.
- It is not a good idea for people to take money home with them, for example, when one plans to make a bank deposit at a later time, or receives a donation off of church property.
- Use church credit cards responsibly.
- Keep and document receipts.

    Keep a copy of all receipts turned in. I was once told to place receipts in our treasurer's open mailbox in the church's main office. I placed a pile of receipts there, and the treasurer never received them. Since I did not make copies, I spent countless hours on the phone getting copies of each receipt from various merchants. Since the receipts were from an out-of-town trip it was quite a challenge. You can always get a copy of a receipt, but it is not always easy. Make your own copies! It is good to have a backup.

Helpful Hint

It is important to be as specific as possible about the items on the receipt. As a youth minister you may buy unusual things for games, so listing the purpose of each item is critical.

I was once called into the church administrator's office to explain why I had purchased personal items on the church credit card. I had no idea what she was talking about. She showed me the receipt where I'd purchased ten pairs of panty hose. Youth ministers often buy strange items for games, but the church administrator had some concerns when she noticed many pairs of panty hose purchased on the church's credit card. I was asked to explain exactly how we were using panty hose in youth ministry. I quickly listed all the games I'd planned for at our summer kickoff that would use the stockings. We both had a great laugh. I did not mind being asked. It was her job to ask, and it was a good reminder of how the church held each staff member accountable. Remember, it is the person's job to ask questions. This does not mean she or he distrusts someone. Clarification is a good thing. Churches have audits, and clarity is important. If you are working for a small church, ask the pastor to recommend someone in the church to help you with finances. This could be the church treasurer or bookkeeper. This person can also help you understand your budget and how to stay within it.

Receipts

I currently give all receipts to my administrative assistant, and she keeps track of them and reconciles the receipts with the bills each month. She is relentless about asking for receipts, and I love it! She makes sure I label each receipt, and is never afraid to question a purchase. We work on this together before every receipt is turned into the financial office. I am so grateful for her help. We celebrate each month when all receipts are turned in. Keeping, finding, and labeling receipts are not my strengths, so I asked for help. It is not just okay to ask for help, it is imperative.

Helpful Hint

Make sure you know what types of expenditures your church allows.

If you are not sure about making a purchase, ask! I learned this one the hard way. I had changed churches and was getting to know some of the youth. I had taken four different youths out to lunch over a period of a few months. The previous church where I had served allowed us to take youth out to lunch or pay for a meal on a church trip. This new church did not allow meals to be charged, and I had no idea of the policy. I just assumed it was okay because it had been allowed at previous churches I had served. I now ask a lot of questions. I am fortunate to be blessed with such a patient church administrator. She is always willing to discuss any budget issue and sends me reminders each month helping me keep within my budget.

Warning!

When you go over budget, the money has to come from a different ministry area. Be a team player. Your youth ministry will not thrive if other ministries aren't doing well.

Stay within your designated budget. I have had generous budgets, and budgets I thought were impossible to stay within. It is important to realize when you go over your budget that the money to make up the difference has to come from another ministry area. The youth ministry of a church cannot thrive without a strong adult and children's ministry. Be a team player, and be respectful of budgets. Look for creative ways to save money. Compare different vendor prices. Use stored items for decorations, or borrow from another ministry in the church or another church. Consider going on a mission trip or retreat with another church. Ask for donations or sponsors for youth trips or retreats. Know your church's policy on fund-raising. Some churches do not allow fund-raising at all while others do not permit youth or children to sell items to raise money. You can usually find this information in an employee handbook or by discussing this in your interview.

Where the Buck Stops

Never accept payments outside of your office or without two people present. It is too easy to put in a pocket of your clothing, a purse, or a book and forget about it. I have had people try to pay me for an event in the middle of the grocery store. I politely say I cannot accept any form of payment outside my office, inform them of our operating hours, and give the person directions for where the office is located. They are usually happy with the information and understand the rule.

Remember it is the job of the administrator or church treasurer to ask questions about budget issues.

It is important not to be defensive. Be willing and prepared to answer questions concerning spending practices, receipts, and so forth. They can and will be great resources for learning. Respect their positions.

Know the policies and procedures for handling money before you begin the job so that you are aware of all expectations.

If you do not want to wave the white flag of defeat, read on.

Double Red Flag

Sex

There is nothing that will sabotage a ministry faster than a sex scandal.

If you are single, be careful of your dating practices. It is difficult to say do not date within the church. Many young people in ministry find church the only way to meet people. Therefore, it is very important how you handle dating. It is best not to introduce people you are casually dating to the youth. They can become attached and feel abandoned if the person you are dating suddenly stops participating. It is not wise to date one of your volunteers, because you will show that person more attention than you realize, and youth and parents will notice. This can also create division among your volunteer team. Do not make any relationship official on a social network before you have announced it to your volunteer team and parents. Think of them as your family. They want to hear this information from you personally.

It is not wise to have an overnight guest of the opposite sex even if she or he is just a friend. This can cause rumors, and much of your time and energy will be spent trying to explain yourself. Yes, it is a different world, but you do have a separate set of standards you must live by whether you think it is fair or not.

Be extremely careful who you share your personal life with. You may also want to be careful about going on blind dates with relatives of people in the congregation. I spent more than a year trying to explain to a very sweet grandmother that I had nothing in common with her grandson. Her grandson felt we had a lot in common and wanted to continue dating. I was just not interested, and she was very insulted. My relationship with her became awkward. It is best to try to meet someone you may be set up with in a casual setting before making any commitment to an official date.

Keep relationships with the members of your volunteer team professional. If you must meet with a committee chairperson who is of the opposite sex, it is best to have another person present. Meet in a public place during the day or in your office with a door open or windows that provide a complete view of your office. Never meet in secret.

> ## Warning!
>
> Do not even think about dating a member of your youth group.

My first job as a youth minister was a summer position at a small church four hours from my home. I lived with a senior adult and was told to start a youth program. The staff of the church consisted of a part-time pastor and me. I was eighteen years old, away from home, and living with a senior adult. She was a wonderful host, and the congregation was amazing, but I had no idea how difficult it would be serving there while not knowing anyone my age. I did not expect to become so lonely over the ten weeks I served there. The youth group became my friends, and one of the male members of the youth group and I became best friends. We never went out on a date, and I cannot think of a time we were alone, but our relationship was definitely different from the relationship I had with the other youth. No one ever questioned our relationship, or said a word about it, but I knew in my mind it was wrong. The age difference was minimal, but my position in the church made the relationship wrong. It was not until years later that I realized the jealousy and hurt it caused in that youth group. They were amazing young people, and many are leaders in their churches today. I felt like they deserved more from their youth minister and I have regretted not being the example I should have been. I have kept in touch with several members from the group, and I have received a lot of grace for my mistake. This situation could have ended much worse, and my ministry to youth could have ended before it really started. I will always be grateful to my friend who was, and still is, a gentleman.

I chose to tell that story about my mistake because the stories of some of my friends and colleagues were just too painful to write. I have watched some of the most outstanding youth ministers leave the youth ministry because of sexual misconduct. I have seen families and congregations suffer the consequences. It is never too late to establish habits and policies for your ministry. Here are a few:

- Establish boundaries now.
- Find a friend you can talk to who will hold you accountable.
- Do not have a romantic relationship with a youth or youth leader/volunteer.
- Never try to council someone of the opposite sex about the person's marriage. Refer him or her to a professional counselor.

- Make sure your office door has a window and someone is within sight when you are meeting someone there alone. Never meet with youth behind a closed door without another adult who can see into the room.
- Protect yourself, your youth, and your congregation.

You can also refer to chapter 8, "The 411 on Avoiding 911," for more information.

The Serpent in the Keyboard

It is important to recognize the temptations of the Internet. Of course we all know computers and other electronic means of communication are useful tools in providing effective ministry, but we must also recognize the unique risk electronic communication presents:

- Assume all Internet usage on a church computer is monitored. All correspondence and documents are property of the church.
- Church computers that are set up for guests or program participants to access the Internet should be in high-traffic places and randomly monitored by staff. Controls should be in place to prevent access to inappropriate content.

Do not share too much information about your relationship on any social network. Parents do not want to read the pet names you and the person you're dating use or how the person you are dating "rocks your world." No one will tell you this, but trust me, everyone thinks it. If you choose to even allow one parent or one staff member to join your friend list, you must be careful about what you write and the pictures you display.

If you choose to accept youth as friends on any social network, or if you text a youth or parent at any time, always be aware every text should be worded carefully. Humor and sarcasm do not translate well in 160 characters or less. Messages can be taken out of context. Always assume everything you write or text is visible to everyone.

Waving the Green Flag: Okay Now but Proceed with Caution

The Green-Eyed Monster

My great-uncle called me a "green-eyed monster" when I was a young child. I had no idea what it meant. He was a very kind man, so I never even considered it might be something negative. It was not until I was older that I understood that "green-eyed monster" referred to jealousy. It did not surprise me because I certainly was jealous of my younger sister, who is the baby of the family.

I have attended countless youth ministry conferences and conventions. At every conference or convention the introductions are the same. They consist of three questions:

1. Where are you from?
2. What church do you serve?
3. How large is your youth group?

I remember the first youth ministry convention I attended after I moved from First United Methodist Church in Hendersonville, North Carolina, to Indian River City United Methodist Church in Titusville, Florida. I no longer had "First" in the name of my church. It was like I had lost a status symbol. The churches were the same size, but it did not sound the same. When you told anyone the name of your church, the reply was always "oh," but the tone was different when you had the word *first* in your church's name.

The numbers game always follows the name game. "How many kids do you have in your youth group?" That is a tricky question. Do they want to know how many we have on the church roll, or the mode, median, or mean? Most youth directors think of every student on the roll and add the students who have passed by on their bikes, plus the occasional skateboarder, and the UPS guy because he looked young. (Okay, maybe that was just me, but it seemed like everyone else did it too.) I always felt like I had to say some huge number to feel validated in my ministry. I also found myself not only jealous of the thousands of youth flocking to other churches, but of their adult volunteer teams. I was especially envious of the leaders who brought their entire volunteer team to the event with matching T-shirts or polo shirts. The next wave of jealousy was of the leaders who had their own youth building or campus. I can remember when my office was next to the preschool, and the youth rooms were on the third floor with no elevator leading to them, and air-conditioning that sometimes seemed to forget the top floor existed. The idea of a "youth ministry campus" was just too much for me to imagine.

I finally realized after about fifteen years in ministry that I did not have to play the numbers game or be envious of volunteer teams or facilities. I no longer allowed the "green-eyed monster" to accompany me on these trips. I found after many years of experience in youth ministry that it is not the number of youth on the roster, the building that you work in each day, or the matching shirts on the volunteer team that makes you an effective youth minister. I realized that effectiveness stems from your love for Christ, passion for ministry, and your willingness to submit to God's will over status, accolades, or personal achievement. Hold on to those things, and you will be an effective youth minister, regardless of the name of your church, the size of your youth group, or the facilities your church provides. Embrace where you are. There is no time, or room, for jealousy.

Flexibility Does Not Mean a Lack of Accountability

There are many night meetings and weekend events in ministry. This usually means you have a little flexibility in your daytime schedule. It is easy to take advantage of the flexibility, and not have office hours at all. I know this is especially tempting when there are only a few other staff members, your office is in a completely different building, or you feel no one holds you accountable for checking in with the office.

It is important to have set office hours each day. People need to know how to reach you and when they can see you. If you have a church secretary or administrative assistant, always let her or him know where you are and when you plan to return. Not knowing your schedule places that person in a difficult position when people call, and she or he has no idea where you are and what you are doing. Flexible hours do not mean you do not have to be in your office. Ask for clear expectations of office hours when you are hired. It is also very important to return e-mails and phone calls in a timely manner.

Meet deadlines! Remember when you miss a deadline for a newsletter article, bulletin announcement, and so on that this makes someone else's job more difficult. Be considerate of other staff members and volunteers, and keep their time constraints in mind as well. Of course, there may be times when you cannot meet a certain deadline. When this happens, let the people whom it will affect know you may be late. You must also be gracious and understanding if they cannot wait for your article. They have deadlines as well. If they can take your contribution after the deadline, it is important to thank them. Do not take advantage of someone's kindness. If you have trouble in this area, there are several ways you can avoid being late. Many phones and computers have reminder systems. Use them. I am not a computer person, but I have a reminder that pops up each week reminding me about articles and deadlines. It has been extremely helpful to me. You can also set aside time each week to set your weekly schedule and review what must be done that week. Checklists are great. My friends and fellow staff members call me "old school" because I like a written calendar and I like to write my to-do list in a spiral notebook. It works for me. Find what works best for you.

Burnout

It is odd for me to talk about burnout to people who are beginning their ministry, but this is when it should be discussed.

There are healthy habits you can learn in the beginning of your ministry that will affect how you minister for the rest of your life.

1. You must be growing in your own faith to help others grow in theirs.

    a. Spend time in prayer.

    b. Participate in a Bible study with your peers. (Do not teach. Participate.)

    c. Worship!

2. Take time to rest.

    a. Take your days off.

    b. Take a vacation.

    c. Do not go into the office on your day off, or spend it catching up on your work. Ministry is wonderful, and youth ministry is so much fun at times you can forget you are working. This can be bad because you will not even recognize how exhaustion is creeping up on you. Once exhaustion reaches you, resentment is not far behind. You will be tired; then you will resent all you are doing. You may even start resenting other people. The deadly force of apathy will join your resentments, and you will be heading for burnout. Many people take this as a sign to change churches when it is really a signal for you to rest, reevaluate how you are doing ministry, and examine how well you delegate and utilize the help and expertise of others. You will also be much more sensitive to others when you are tired. You may feel hurt, unappreciated, or unneeded. Rest can help you avoid all of these triggers for burnout. This sounds so simple, but I have to admit this is one of the most difficult things I deal with.

3. Refuel

   a. Attend a conference or a retreat each year to help you learn new ideas and approaches to ministry. If this is not financially possible, attend a day training event.

b. Get to know other youth ministers in your area. Meet once a month for lunch. Exchange ideas, concerns, and information. Offer and receive encouragement.

c. Avoid the numbers game. Remember it is a game you cannot win.

d. Read books or articles that help keep you excited about ministry.

My prayer is that you realize when you are in a dangerous current, will know when you need to stay out of the water, recognize when you should swim parallel to the shore, and acknowledge the moments when you need to simply soak in God's grace.

Chapter 4

Never Let Them See You Sweat
Recruiting and Leading Adult Volunteers

We have this idea that everyone who feels called to youth ministry knows their calling and acts on it. We tend to think announcements in church where we beg people to serve or a blurb in the Sunday morning bulletin are enough to motivate people to volunteer for positions they know very little about. Save your energy and your paper. Recruiting volunteers is not like searching for a needle in a haystack (which it sometimes feels like). It is about helping people discover their gifts and equipping them to serve. It is actually my second favorite part of my job. I love helping people find their place to serve and then equipping them for the service. The word *equipping* may be new to you. It was new to me until I read the book *The Equipping Church* by Sue Mallory (Zondervan, 2001). It helped me redefine recruiting and training as helping people find their gifts, then training them to use those gifts. You must start by not being afraid to set the bar high for volunteers. Never ask for less than the best of the best!

A Call to Serve

How do you discern someone's call to serve? Observe and ask questions. Observe adults and how they interact with teens. Adult volunteers should be well grounded and growing in their faith. They should also be mature. Maturity does not necessarily mean older. Some college students are more mature than some parents. Here are some helpful questions to ask yourself:

- Are they good role models?
- Can they talk about their faith openly?
- Do they have a sense of humor?
- Are they flexible?
- What is their leadership style?

Do not expect every adult to be perfect or you will have a difficult time building a volunteer team. Your team needs to be diverse. The best teams consist of adults who are married, unmarried, older, and younger (over the age of twenty-one).

Try to bring together a group of volunteers that includes people with various personality types. You do not need an entire team of extroverted young people. This may be fun, but getting things done will be like herding cats, and being around so many extroverts will be overwhelming to teens who are introverted. Look at your own personality type. You should strive to find people who balance you and one another. For example, I am an extrovert who always sees the big picture. It is important for me to have people on my team who pay close attention to details. They keep me well grounded and on track. I know where my weaknesses are, and I look to find people who are strong in those areas. Do not be threatened by people who have gifts in the areas you do not. They will be an asset to you and will strengthen the ministry.

If you have some volunteers who are under the age of twenty-one, it is better to pair them with someone older. Try to have those under twenty-one work primarily with middle school youth. Determine on an individual basis what to do with volunteers younger than twenty-one. Some will be more mature than others. It is better for there to be some age difference between the volunteer leaders and teens. Some eighteen-year-olds who have graduated high school feel the need or want to remain in the youth group and volunteer as leaders. It may be difficult for them to make the transition, so you will need to be clear about your expectations. Know the youth protection policies of your church. Some churches do not allow anyone under the age of twenty-one to volunteer with youth. You can refer to chapter 8 of this manual if you have questions about youth protection.

Ask for Input

Ask teens whom they would like to have as leaders. Each year I send out a survey to all youth. I ask them to list topics they would like to discuss, to suggest ideas to make the youth ministry stronger, to tell me what they enjoy most, and to list adults they would like to see as leaders. This can be done electronically, through the mail, or at a youth event. Decide what works best for you.

Ask pastors and church leaders. This is especially important if you are new to a church. Take their opinions seriously. Sometimes a pastor may not be able to reveal why someone would not be a good leader because the pastor is involved or has been involved in counseling with that person. You should still take your pastor's advice even if the pastor cannot divulge confidential information.

Recruiting Parents

Negotiations

There we were, sitting face-to-face. I looked her straight in the eyes, being careful not to blink. Could she see the fear in my eyes? I said to myself, "Stay calm. Do not let her see you

sweat. She cannot know you are desperate."
She looked away for what seemed like an eter-
nity, then tilted her head to the left and said,
"Whatever." Whatever? What kind of answer
was that? I was prepared for "No." I had prepared quite the argument for a no. I had no
idea what to do with a "whatever." This sev-
enth-grade girl was no ordinary youth. I had
met my match. She may have mastered the
art of negotiation at the age of twelve, but I
had age and experience on my side. I was not
going to let her see me sweat. I remained calm
and slowly asked the question again. "May I
ask your parents to serve on the leadership
team for the youth group?" I needed a defini-
tive answer. I waited. She responded with a
question. "Why do you want my parents?"
Aha! Negotiations were still open!

Let's face it, no one wants to negotiate with a middle school girl, but that may be your toughest obstacle
in recruiting volunteers to work with youth. Parental
involvement is vital if you want to have a successful youth
ministry. You can avoid resentment and earn respect by
asking teens for their permission to invite a parent or
parents to serve.

Why Parents?

Parents have the largest investment already in the youth ministry—their child. Parents should have a fundamental role in the spiritual development of their teen. Parents give the youth ministry a higher value of respect in the church. Because parents network with other parents, they will be your strongest advocates and marketers.

You will have better participation on trips and retreats if parents serve as leaders, chaperones, and so on.

Helpful Hint

Parents are more likely to trust other parents.

Why Ask Teens for Permission?

Teens need to feel ownership in the ministry. Asking for permission shows respect for a teen's space. The conversation with the teens in your group will give you an opportunity to communicate. It can be very affirming for a teen to hear why you feel her or his parent(s) should serve in a leadership position. It helps teens to know and understand parents are not the enemy. When teens feel comfortable communicating with youth leaders who are parents, it helps them communicate more effectively with their own parents.

What if the Teen Says No?

If a teen doesn't want his or her parents to volunteer, try to negotiate. Here are some suggestions:

- If your group is divided by age/grade, ask if the teen's parents can help with another age level or grade.
- If the answer is still no, then respect his or her wishes, but remind the teen that you may be asking again in a year.
- Ask again in a year.

Warning

Youth ministry leadership should not be limited to parents. It should be open to anyone who feels the *call to serve* and has the *ability to lead* effectively.

Asking for TIPS

I am not afraid to ask anyone who I feel has the TIPS needed to make them assets in the youth ministry program. (TIPS is an acronym for "trainable," "inspirational," "prayerful," and "servant-hearted.")

- Trainable

  Look for people who are open and willing to receive training for the position. If a person has a heart for God and a heart for youth, everything else can be learned. I truly believe this. Training is the key. If a person is willing to be trained in child protection and that person's area of service, then I am willing to provide the best training possible. I love to learn, and I love people who are willing to learn. If a person feels he or she does not need any training and is not willing to be taught our policies and procedures, I do not feel he or she is the right person for our team.

- Inspirational

  Look for people who inspire others with their words and actions. Leaders should have strong relationships with Jesus and be willing to be inspirations to others. These volunteers will be well grounded in their faith and have the respect of the congregation. They must also be willing to inspire youth to learn and grow in their faith. Inspirational people in your congregation are easy to find. They have attended or led adult Bible studies. They can be motivational but not necessarily outgoing. They can be "gentle giants" who lead quietly and consistently by living their faith, or well-respected sports coaches who show their love of Christ though their love of family and friends. My best leaders are people I enjoy being with and can learn from.

• Prayerful

Look for people who have a strong faith and who communicate with Jesus. You may have someone who has no children or grandchildren in the program, who may not even really like children or feel comfortable around them, but if the person has a heart to help because she or he feels that youth are an important part of the family of God, you can find a place for her or him. If someone feels that prayer is her or his spiritual gift, consider creating a prayer group.

Discuss how important confidentiality is and develop a covenant not to speak of prayer requests outside the group. Share concerns from the youth, upcoming events, and even personal requests with the group. Knowing there are people who pray for you and the youth will give you strength and peace in times of need. It will make a tremendous difference in the ministry. Prayer warriors can also be teachers, helpers, and chaperones, but those positions are best for those who like children and enjoy being around them.

Pray and seek God's guidance before you ask anyone to serve in a leadership position. Continue to pray for your ministry team throughout members' terms of service. Ask how you can pray for them and remind them often that they are being surrounded by prayer.

- Servant-hearted

  Look for people who see themselves as serving others, not themselves. Not every volunteer has the heart of a servant, and some can be difficult to work with. This presents any youth leader with a challenge. Avoid challenging situations by recruiting people to be on the ministry team who have the hearts of servants. Some people want to work with youth because they want to be young again; some want to play but not have responsibilities; and some want to make sure the ministry goes the way they want it to go. They usually have their own agendas that are not compatible with the mission of the ministry.

  You can usually tell if a person has the heart of a servant by the answers the person gives to the list of interview guidelines for employees and volunteers found in this chapter. Carefully consider the answers to the questions

dealing with forgiveness and working within a group or team. People
who have the hearts of servants are
willing to give and accept forgiveness, and work with a group or
team. They are open to new ideas
and do not mind if they have no title
or receive little recognition. The success of the ministry serves as their
recognition.

Servant-hearted volunteers are
like precious jewels to any leader.
They are the most valuable volunteers, and you should cherish
them. Surround yourself with these
people and consistently let them
know how valuable they are. They
may not *need* to hear it but they will
appreciate hearing it.

Getting the Best Volunteers

Make It Personal

One-on-one, personal communication always works
best for recruiting volunteers. It is also best to ask people
face-to-face. You may call and ask them to meet with
you individually over coffee, ice cream, lunch, or in your

office. Give them clear expectations about time commitment, training, and leadership. Provide a detailed job description and any other resources you have available such as an adult volunteer manual. Give each person time to pray about his or her decision. Ask any who accept the volunteer position to serve for one month, then meet with each volunteer again to decide if the position is right for him or her. This gives you both the opportunity to say if the position is right for him or her. It is very difficult to "fire" a volunteer. It is better to decide if things are working out in the beginning.

Volunteer List

Create a volunteer list. Since I am a very visual person, I like to make a chart. The chart basically lists the position to be filled, qualifications/expectations, a list of people who qualify for that position, and the lucky person who accepts the position.

Position	Qualifications/Expectations	Candidates	Filled by

Volunteer positions range from long-term commitments such as Sunday school teachers to short-term commitments such as mission trip fund-raiser or retreat counselor.

Interview and evaluate every person who wants to work with youth or children.

Interview Guidelines for Employees and Volunteers

There are a number of interview questions that can help determine the motives behind why people want to work or volunteer with children. Ask these questions and keep notes to help you in the volunteer and/or employment process.

- Tell me about yourself. (This begins the interview with a nonthreatening, open-ended question.)
- Summarize your employment history. (Look for frequent moves, gaps in employment, and reasons for termination. If you are looking for a reliable volunteer or employee, this question will give you valuable information.)
- Tell me about your experience with youth. Have you worked or volunteered for other children's or youth organizations? (Watch for adults whose lives seem to revolve around spending time with children or youth.)

- What strengths can you bring to this job or position?
- Why do you want to work with youth? (Watch to see if the candidate is too focused on the youth or wants to work with children because they are "pure," "innocent," "trusting," "nonjudgmental," "clean," and so on. Adults should want to work with the youth because they have something to offer the teens. Be aware of the adults who want to work with youth because youth meet adult needs.)
- What do you do in your spare/leisure time? Tell me about your hobbies or interests. (Watch for people who want to spend their free time with children or youth and have hobbies that are more appealing to youth than adults. For example, it is okay for an adult to enjoy playing video games with youth, but adults should have adult friends and participate in adult activities. If a person is immersed in the world of teens it may be because she or he has not reached the maturity level of an adult. This may be due to fear. It is important to offer the person ways to grow in her or his faith with other adults and build adult relationships.)

- What ages of children or youth do you prefer to work with? (Watch for a candidate who only wants to work with a specific age. It is okay for people to have a preference, but listen carefully if a person *only* wants to work with one age group. A negative example of this might be: "I like working with youth because I can 'control' them." It is never good to put someone in a leadership position who is seeking control. Listen for continual "I want" or "I need" statements. You want volunteers who are focused on the needs of teens, not their own needs. Challenge the person to step out of his or her comfort zone and teach another age group. See if the person is open to seeing a personal gift within that he or she may not have recognized before or if the person shuts down because of not getting his or her way.)

- Do you have any reservations about working with teens of different ages? (It is okay if candidates have reservations. The important thing here is listening to see if they are willing to express their reservations or if they get nervous when you ask the question. People who are comfortable with themselves are able to admit what challenges them.)

- Do you think there are any reasons to treat boys and girls differently? (Listen closely to their responses and rationale. Do the answers feel right?)

- How were you disciplined as a child? Do you feel the discipline was appropriate? (Note if the family resolved problems by physical punishment.)

- What do you consider acceptable discipline? (Avoid adults who need control.)

- How do you deal with stress? (Look for positive outlets for stress such as exercising, scrapbooking, or taking time out for themselves. Be aware of people who say they do not have stress, or they punch walls. [I actually had someone tell me this once.] You do not want anyone to ever use violence to handle stress.)

- What is your plan for dealing with stress?

- What makes you angry? (Avoid people who cannot admit they have been angry. Look for people to be real. However, if they can immediately give you long lists of things that make them angry, you will most likely be on those lists soon.)

RED FLAG!

Beware if someone says, "I don't like people telling me how to do my job or correcting me" or "I love children but their parents drive me crazy." People who lead youth must be able to relate to parents.

- If you saw another teacher/staff/volunteer—one whom you like and respect—showing acts of aggression with a youth, such as striking a youth, what would you do? (Make sure that at some point the candidate knows to tell a supervisor or pastor.)
- Have you ever been reprimanded at work? For what? (Was the person's reprimand related to dealing with youth?)
- Who are your best friends? (Adults' best friends should be other adults.)
- Do you relate better with children and youth or adults? (Be cautious of anyone who relates better with children or youth than she or he does with adults.)
- How do you feel you can best serve the youth of our congregation and community?

- Do you like working within a group or alone?
- Can you share examples of when you have given and when you have received forgiveness?

Training Volunteers

When people are given jobs, they want to know the purpose of the job, their responsibilities, and what resources are available to help them serve in the best way possible. Training should be informative, productive, and fun. Leaders need to feel equipped and empowered after training. Always let attendees evaluate training sessions they attend.

Leaders should not just be trained annually in youth protection, they should be offered training in dealing with discipline, teaching techniques, recognizing age-level characteristics, and strengthening spiritual development. There are many resources listed at the end of this chapter that can help you with training.

Hosting a Training Event: The Meal

I consider training a meal. There should be an appetizer, meat, side dish, and dessert.

THE APPETIZER. The appetizer *is* actually food. Every volunteer training event begins with food. That is my appetizer. It may be a snack, brunch, lunch, or dinner. It does not have to be expensive or extravagant, but being creative never hurts. You can choose a theme or just a theme color.

THE MEAT. The meat is the core of the training. Give volunteers what they need! Everyone should receive a job description with her or his purpose and responsibilities—as well as expectations—listed. Each person should be given curriculum (if applicable), and access to all resources needed to serve in her or his position. For example, if you are training Sunday school leaders you would give them class lists with contact information, tours of their classrooms, curriculum, teacher guides, youth protection policies, and show them where to find supplies. If you are training for vacation Bible school you would present the theme, introduce curriculum, list the schedule, and so on. All volunteers who work directly with youth should receive youth protection training as well as training in age-appropriate discipline. This would be the meat of the training.

THE SIDE DISH. The side dish would be additional resources offered to anyone who may want them. A resource table filled with Bible maps, devotional books, Bible dictionaries, posters, and so forth is always appreciated at a Sunday school or vacation Bible school training session.

THE DESSERT. The dessert is the theme, decorations, or the fun part of the event. It can be as simple as placing a dot on the back of one chair and giving a door prize to the person who sits there or decorating the entire room in a theme, complete with music and costumes. You can be as creative as you wish with your training, but make sure your focus does not get lost in the theme.

Always invite your pastor(s) to attend or participate in volunteer training. If you are not comfortable training volunteers, your pastor(s) may be willing to provide the training or help you find a qualified person to lead.

Provide evaluations for participants to fill out listing ways future trainings could be improved.

Here are a few job description samples you may use to help train your leaders:

Job Description: Teacher

The purpose of your role is to plan and implement weekly lessons that will provide each teen with an opportunity to learn and grow in faith and to nurture each of the youth so that she or he will experience the love of Christ through you.

Your Responsibilities Are:

- Read the curriculum and prepare the lesson.
- Verify that the required supplies and resources will be available by contacting the education office early in the week.
- Arrive before the youth (by _____ a.m./p.m.) to arrange the class as you wish and to discuss any ways in which the secretary and helper can assist you.
- Ensure that the guidelines of the youth protection policy are met and request help from the education office if necessary to remain within these guidelines.
- If you are unable to attend on your scheduled Sunday, please contact a substitute as soon as possible and let us know who will be teaching your class.
- Show the love of Christ to each person in your class.

Sunday Morning Contacts and Information:

Name _____

Phone/Cell _____

Location of supply closet if applicable _____

_____

_____

Job Description: Helper/Assistant

The purpose of your role is to assist the Sunday school teacher in the ways that best serve both the teacher and students. You are the extra eyes, ears, and hands for our teachers.

Your Responsibilities Are:

- Arrive to class no later than _____ a.m./p.m. to discuss any specific help the teacher may need for that day.
- Greet each person as he or she comes into the class.
- Provide support by passing out and collecting supplies as needed.
- Contact _____ if additional supplies or helpers are needed.
- If you are unable to attend on your scheduled Sunday, please contact a substitute as soon as possible and let us know who will be helping in your class.
- Show the love of Christ to each youth in your class.

Sunday Morning Contacts:

Name _____

Phone/Cell _____

Job Description: Secretary

The purpose of your role is to support the Sunday school teacher by providing assistance during sign-in time; sending notes to youth for birthdays, special events, and missed Sundays; and calling and reminding parent volunteers.

Your Responsibilities Are:

- Arrive by _____ a.m./p.m.
- Greet the youth as they enter the room.
- Follow the instructions listed in the Sunday school binder.
- Ensure that the guidelines of the youth protection policy are met and request help from the education office if necessary to remain within these guidelines.
- If you are unable to attend on your scheduled Sunday, please contact a substitute as soon as possible and let us know who will be serving in your place.
- Show the love of Christ to each youth in your class.

Sunday Morning Contacts:

To request help or supplies, contact _____

_____

Phone/Cell _____

Sample Forms

Evaluation Form

Name of the Event _____ Date _____

What did you enjoy most? _____

_____

_____

_____

What did you find to be the most challenging? _____

_____

_____

_____

What would you change next year? _____

_____

_____

_____

You can do a rating system and list different elements of the event such as:

Rate each part of the retreat from 1 through 10, with 1 being the lowest rating and 10 being the highest rating.

Music _____ Small-group time _____ Session 1 _____

Worship _____ Schedule _____

Food: Breakfast _____ Lunch _____ Dinner _____

Communication: Church _____ Community _____

Name (optional) _____

May we contact you to be on the planning or leadership team for this event next year? (name, e-mail address, and phone number required) _____

_____

Prayer and Encouragement

Pray for your leaders. Spend time each day praying for each of your leaders by name. Let them know you are praying for them. Encourage them to grow in their faith and to grow as leaders. Thank them for a job well done.

Resources for Youth Volunteers

Doug Fields, *Help! I'm a Volunteer Youth Worker!* (El Cajon, Calif.: Youth Specialties; Grand Rapids: Zondervan, 1992).

Ray Johnston, *Help! I'm a Sunday School Teacher!* (El Cajon, Calif.: Youth Specialties, 1995).

Jonathan R. McKee and Thomas W. McKee, *The New Breed: Understanding and Equipping the Twenty-first-Century Volunteer* (Loveland, Colo.: Group, 2008).

Mark Oestreicher, *Help! I'm a Junior High Youth Worker!* (Grand Rapids: Youth Specialties, 1996).

Chapter 5

Just Give Me the Bare Necessities
Creating and Developing the Ministry

How to or Not to Create a
Student Handbook or Manual

I just unpacked a box of youth handbooks I have given out over the past twenty years, and I have to admit I am quite embarrassed by what I expected teens to read and understand. These old handbooks are full of rules, policies, and way too much information. They look more like poorly written legal documents made up of outdated clip art and bad copies of art. How in the world did I expect youth to read manuals or handbooks like these? The words *manual* or *handbook* send most youth straight into nap mode. I am not saying handbooks or manuals are not necessary for ministry; after all I am a writer of manuals. I see the need, and I do believe there is a need for a short summary of information to be given to teens to help them understand the purpose or mission statement of the youth ministry. It is also important to list the ministries provided for youth. A manual needs to be creative, well written, informative, and fun.

Helpful Hint

Do not be afraid to mix information with fun.

Here are tips to make your student/youth manual or handbook a successful source of information. I hope these ideas get your creative juices flowing.

I. Think of a creative title for your handout.

   A. Text message: Use text messaging abbreviations.

   B. "I-info": There is an app that puts your information on pages that look like an application for a mobile device.

   C. Connect the "dots": Name the sections.

      1. D: Data

      2. O: Objectives

      3. T: Theology

      4. S: Student responsibilities

   D. "Menu for ministry": Design your handbook to resemble a menu or cookbook. This is a full-service menu and youth may order the entire meal or choose á la carte. The ministry is catered to them.

1. Appetizers: entry points such as game nights, movies, lock-ins, concerts, scavenger hunts, etc.

2. Salads: small-group topical studies, introduction to the Bible, etc., or large-group events and worship

3. Vegetables: accountability groups, deeper Bible learning, service projects

4. Meat/Main course: high-commitment Bible studies groups, mission projects, and trips

5. Dessert: serving in a leadership position in the youth group or church

II. What to include in the student manual/handbook

A. Church name, street address, Web address, and telephone numbers

B. Leaders' names and contact information

C. Purpose of your ministry or mission statement (This should be written by your youth and adult leaders under the guidance of the youth minister.)

D. Ministry logo (if you have one)

E. Basic outline of the ministry presented in a creative way

F. If you feel you must include rules and regulations or conduct codes, let the youth write a covenant of behavior together.

    1. You can let youth sign the covenant and include it in your handbook/manual.

    2. You can also have the covenant made into a large poster and place it in your classroom or youth building, or elsewhere on campus.

    3. Youth can sign the poster. Asking new youth to read and autograph the covenant would be a great way to welcome them.

G. Include a very basic outline of the youth ministry schedule. Remember, too much information is overwhelming.

    1. You may want to show the youth additional programs, retreats, fund-raisers, and other events, but instead of being inviting to the students it can be overwhelming. Youth may have a difficult time deciding which activities to attend and when and where to go.

2. Instead of including every event in your handbook, give youth a three-month calendar targeting only their age group. You can provide details about the events and ministries on the back of the calendar.

3. Create or use your existing church Web site to keep youth up to date.

Adult Leaders' Handbook or Manual

My views on adult volunteer manuals are quite different. I never want to frighten away a potential adult volunteer, but I also want to be clear about the responsibilities and expectations.

The manual should be well written, direct, and full of information so it may be used throughout a volunteer's time of service.

This information does not have to be called a manual or handbook. I have heard of creative names and I have used a few. Here are a few to get you started:

- Road Map
- Survival Kit
- Youth Ministry Bible
- Serving for Dummies
- Superhero Handbook

- Backstage Pass
- Even Jesus Had Twelve
- Blueprints for Building Disciples
- Construction Instructions
- A Job Description for the Unpaid and
  Underappreciated (on Earth)

Here are some things to include in your unnamed book, booklet, manual, stack of stapled papers, and so forth.

1. An introduction that includes information about the youth minister and the youth ministry written by the youth minister.

   Kirk Dana, adjunct professor of youth ministry at Florida Southern College, and minister to students at First United Methodist Church of Lakeland, Florida, begins his manual, which he calls a "Blueprint," with a personal letter. He introduces himself, and shares the ministry purpose, vision, and goals. He ends his letter by requesting parents and leaders to pray for him and for one another. I think that is a wonderful way to begin your "whatever you call it" because it makes it personal and informative.

2. Job descriptions.

   Include job descriptions for all volunteer leaders. Be as clear and precise as possible. It is important to include a description for all volunteer positions so each volunteer is aware of her or his responsibilities and the responsibilities of others, such as interns (paid and unpaid), assistants, associate ministers, or directors.

3. Safety and appropriate contact guidelines or youth protection policies and procedures.

   Every leader should have a copy from his or her initial recruiting and training, but it is always good to include this in the manual for review and reference. The number for the national child abuse hotline should be included in every manual. The National Child Abuse Hotline number is 1-800-4-A-CHILD (1-800-422-4453).

4. Discipline guidelines.

   Leaders need to know when and how to discipline. They also should be given a clear understanding of when they should go directly to the youth minister for assistance. Discipline guidelines should be unique to each church. There are several ways to establish your guidelines.

   a. Collect guidelines from several youth ministers in your area. Urban churches may have different discipline issues from rural churches.

   b. Ask volunteer youth leaders and youth to help establish discipline guidelines.

5. Scripture and quotes to inspire and motivate.

Here are a couple of examples:

Now all things are of God, who has reconciled us to Himself through Jesus Christ and has given us the ministry of reconciliation, that is, that God was in Christ reconciling the world to Himself, not imputing their trespasses to them, and has committed to us the word of reconciliation. Now then, we are ambassadors for Christ, as though God were pleading through us: we implore you on Christ's behalf, be reconciled to God. For He made Him who knew no sin to be sin for us, that we might become the righteousness of God in Him.

—2 Corinthians 5:18–20

It isn't easy to stay with Jesus in ministry . . . but we must. Deep in our souls, he's whispering how much he loves us. If we'd just take the time to listen to those words and believe them, then our ministries would be gloriously ruined by Jesus . . . and our souls would no longer be in danger.

—Mike Yaconelli,
Getting Fired for the Glory of God, 18

Layers of Learning

Youth Smell and Make Us Cry

Youth: For your information, there's a lot more to youth than people think.

Youth Leader: Example?

Youth: Example? . . . Uh . . . Youth are like onions.

Youth Leader: They stink?

Youth: Yes. . . . No!

Youth Leader: Oh, they make you cry?

Youth: No!

Youth Leader: Oh, you leave them out in the sun, they get all brown and start sprouting little white hairs . . .

> Youth: (peels an onion) *No!* Layers. Onions have layers. Youth have layers. Onions have layers. You get it? We both have layers.
>
> Youth Leader: Oh you both have *layers.* Oh, you know, not everyone likes youth. What about children? Everybody loves children!
>
> Youth: I don't care what everybody likes.

In case you did not notice, this is actually a conversation between an ogre and a donkey. (I never thought I would write that sentence.) It is adapted from the movie *Shrek.* It is a conversation between Shrek and Donkey as they discuss ogres, but it reminded me so much of working with youth. Just like ogres, youth have layers of learning.

Before you begin thinking about how to plan a lesson you should know some basic layers of learning that an individual experiences.

- Lack of Knowledge: The person does not care about the subject and is not interested in the experience of learning.
- Attentiveness: The person becomes aware of what is being taught and begins to pay attention.

- Interest: The person finds the subject to be interesting but is not sure if it is true.
- Acknowledgment: The subject acknowledges that the subject seems to be true.
- Conviction: The person begins to see the subject is true to the person, and he or she wants it to be true to others.
- Dedication: The person views the subject as very important in one's life.

These layers of learning apply to spirituality.

- Lack of Knowledge: Seeds are planted when there is a lack of knowledge (Matthew 13:3–9, The Parable of the Sower).
- Attentiveness: Attentiveness is the layer of learning where youth pay attention to spiritual matters. However, they are not sure they apply to their lives.
- Interest: At the interest layer, youth are not sure how God, Jesus, and the Holy Spirit are real. But they are interested in how the story could be true.
- Acknowledgment: The acknowledgment layer means a person acknowledges truth but still has doubt.

- Conviction: Youth at the level of conviction have a passion for knowledge and truth, and they want to share information.
- Dedication: At the layer of dedication, youth are loyal and committed. They take what they have been learning and apply it to daily living. This layer is where the most growth occurs.

Layers of Learning within Age Groups

Now that you know the layers of learning, you can combine them with the characteristics of various age groups. This will be beneficial in planning lessons that reach youth in the appropriate way for their level of development.

Middle School

Middle school youth are dealing with changing bodies, changing thought processes (from concrete to abstract), changing schools, and, most likely, changing peer groups. It is an awkward time because nothing seems stable. Small-group ministry works best with this age group, but these youths need large-group interaction as well. A middle school–age youth learns better with a partner, but she or he should not always have the same partner. The small-group atmosphere provides the needed stability, but middle school youth need to travel beyond their comfort zone in a safe environment to form new relationships. They enjoy learning through activities such as games and team building. Lecturing is not usually an effective form of teaching for this age group. The youth should be able to ask questions, participate in discussions, and exchange ideas. They enjoy discussing challenging questions. They are not likely to sit and listen for extended periods of time. This is not showing disrespect. It is just a part of how they learn and develop. Every middle school youth will not be on the same spiritual level or be able to understand symbolic, abstract examples or analogies.

In a nutshell, middle school youth lessons should be taught in small groups (ten to twelve individuals) and given opportunities to move around, ask questions, and give feedback. They do not learn well by completing individual worksheets or projects. Never call on students to read out loud unless they volunteer! Being singled out can be very embarrassing for them. Offer opportunities to interact and learn in large groups for short amounts of time. Small-group Bible studies with large-group worship opportunities work well with this age group. Of course you must always take into account the number of adult volunteers and available space when deciding on youth group sizes.

Example of a One-Hour Middle School Lesson

- Greetings/gathering: 10 minutes

    Have snacks or an activity available. Greet the youth by name and ask questions about school, sports, movies, or music. Adult leaders should engage in conversation.

    Divide youth into small groups: 5 minutes

    Divide each group into smaller groups if necessary. Groups should have at least three people and no more than six.

- Small-group Bible study: 15 minutes

    Provide a different translation of the Bible for each group or use the same translation. Ask someone in the group to volunteer to be the reader or all group participants may take turns. Provide each group with a large piece of paper and markers. Ask each group to summarize what they thought was important about the passage.

- Small-group sharing: 10 minutes

  Let each group tell about what they read. They can choose one spokesperson or several spokespeople. Assist them in learning the art of taking turns.

- Summary discussion: 5 minutes

  Come together as a group and summarize what they have learned and ask them how they could apply that Scripture to their lives.

- Prayer time: 5 minutes

  Ask for prayer concerns. Spend the remaining time listing the concerns on a board or bookmarks that can be given out and have each youth write down the concerns to take home. It is always good to ask for praises for what has happened over the week as well.

- Close in prayer.

There are many great resources for middle school youth listed in the back of the book.

High School

High school youth are searching for who they are and who they are going to be. They are very influenced by their peers. They need strong role models who practice what they preach. They watch and listen. They are not afraid to challenge authority, but they also strive to fit in. They enjoy active games and activities. Every activity does not have to be competitive. At this age they want to learn to solve problems, but high school youth can become easily frustrated. They want authentic leadership and deeper knowledge of the Bible. They want strong friendships that require more than just a click on a social network site. They want to be alike and different at the same time. They crave positive attention. High school youth love asking the tough questions. They want to know how to put their biblical knowledge into action. They love exchanging ideas and feel frustrated when they are not taken seriously. High school students do not come to church for programs. They come because of their spiritual hunger and to form and grow relationships. They need time to socialize with their peers as well as time to interact with leaders. High school leaders should have spiritual depth and a passion for missions, service, and ministry. High school students want to serve. Do not be afraid to give high school youth leadership roles, but remember they need a place to grow spiritually with their peers as well. They ask tough questions, and they need leaders who are willing to discuss the tough topics both biblically and socially. The youth minister and volunteer leaders should be accessible and approachable.

It is difficult to give just one example of a high school lesson because there are various levels of lessons/studies at this stage. Some high school youth are ready for high commitment studies that require outside reading, weekly attendance, and accountability. Other students are in need of topical Bible studies or short-term series. You can refer to the Appendix B at the end of this manual for curriculum ideas.

Allow high school students to help develop the high school ministry. High school students are most likely to stay involved in a ministry where they have some ownership. Make them partners in your ministry.

Not All Waterslides Lead to God, but Some Do

Sherri McKelvin became a missionary in the seventh grade. I am sure she was not aware of her position as a missionary because she was quite shy, and in seventh grade you believe all missionaries have to live in a hut in Africa.

Sherri was a missionary in Etowah, North Carolina. Her mission field was a public school bus. Sherri and I sat together each morning and afternoon. It worked perfectly. She was quiet, and I was very "social." Well, there we were each day sitting together chatting away about every subject under the sun. Actually, *I* was chatting away. Sherri was very polite, smiled a lot, and was a great listener. She did, however, always manage to extend to me an invitation each morning and each afternoon. She always invited me to church. Sherri lived three doors down from the Baptist church, and I lived about a quarter mile away from Sherri. The church was well within walking distance, but I did not really know that much about church. I had attended a few vacation Bible schools as a child, and they were quite wonderful. But my family did not attend church, so my interest was quite minimal. I also had this crazy idea that you had to pay to go to church. Our family did not have a lot of money, so I always politely declined her invitation until the last day of school. On the last day of school the invitation changed. It was not an invitation to church but to a waterslide, and it was *free*! Now that caught my attention. Who could say no to a waterslide? It was my first youth group trip. I went to the waterslide and felt welcomed by the other youth. I began walking to church each Sunday morning, Sunday night, and Wednesday night. Etowah Baptist Church is where I found God and received my call to ministry. Not all waterslides lead to God, but some do!

Building a Well-Balanced Youth Ministry

Day Trips, Camps, Retreats, Neighborhood Outreach, Movies, and So On

It is important to have trips and retreats that are open to new youth. Encourage youth to invite their friends, and help them learn and practice hospitality. Fun trips, retreats, movie nights, and so on are great places for youth to enter the church. There should be many opportunities throughout the year for new youth to attend. Make events free if possible or have a scholarship/sponsorship program for any youth in need. I prefer to use the word *sponsorship*. Be discreet in how youth scholarships/sponsorships are dispersed, so youth are not embarrassed. Do not abandon your neighborhood. Think of ways to invite youth from your neighborhood to be a part of your church, and, most of all, to join the family of God.

Community Building

Youth need opportunities to create and participate in a community. This can be achieved through group games, parties, or dances. These events are usually held on the church campus in order to help youth feel comfortable at church. These activities should offer opportunities for youth to communicate easily, and good communication skills should be modeled by your leaders. There should always be a greeter or greeters at every entrance. It is important to learn the names of the youth and call them by name. Youth usually do not like to use nametags, but it is the easiest way for everyone to learn names. You may want to give candy to everyone with a legible nametag and/or a prize for the most creative nametag decorations.

Spiritual Growth

Bible studies should be offered on several levels. This includes, but is not limited to, small-group topical Bible studies, accountability groups, Scripture studies, prayer groups, and large-group worship experiences. These are opportunities for youth to learn Scripture and how to apply it to their daily lives. Do not forget prayer. Encourage youth at this stage to keep prayer journals. It will be a wonderful way for them to see how God is at work in their lives.

Commitment

When a group of youth hungers for spiritual growth and wants to dive deep into Scripture or theology, it is important to meet the need. High-commitment Bible studies that require reading outside the classroom, meeting attendance goals, and participating in class are a great way to meet this need. This is usually offered to high school students. Ask youth to commit to pray for one another and the church, and to offer concerns and praises for themselves and others. This stage of youth ministry could also include accountability groups where students discuss what is going on in their lives and hold one another accountable for prayer, study, and conduct. You will never do anyone a favor by expecting too little of him or her.

Service

This can include service projects within the church and throughout the community. Mission trips and spiritual retreats based on serving others are wonderful ways to teach and model serving. Youth should have several opportunities throughout the year to serve others.

Here are a few examples of service opportunities:

- Youth can sponsor a child in another country through an organization such as Compassion International, World Vision, Save the Children, or Christian Foundation for Children. There are many other groups you can research.

- Youth can visit retirement homes or nursing homes. They can sing, visit, take small gifts, decorate doors or hallways for holidays, assist with repairs, read books, or donate items.
- Many children's ministers need youth helpers for vacation Bible school or other summer activities for children.
- Make snack bags and deliver them to family waiting areas at the local hospital.
- Decorate senior adult homes for the holidays.
- Offer to host a computer class for senior adults. Help them set up their laptops and show them how to use social media. Your church must have Wi-Fi access for this to work.
- Write letters or cards to homebound members of your congregation. Follow up by visiting them in small groups.
- Spend a day volunteering at a soup kitchen, homeless shelter, community clothes closet, or animal shelter.
- Look for needs specific to your community and how you can help children and youth in your local area. Be creative.

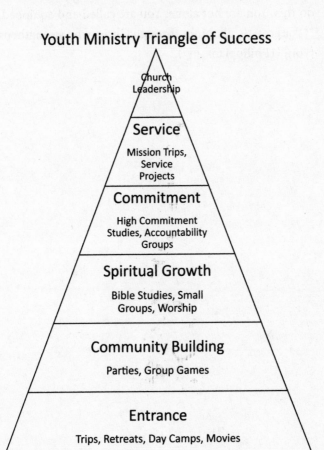

Youth Ministry Triangle of Success

Church
Leadership

Service
**Mission Trips,
Service
Projects**

Commitment
**High Commitment
Studies, Accountability
Groups**

Spiritual Growth
**Bible Studies, Small
Groups, Worship**

Community Building
Parties, Group Games

Entrance
Trips, Retreats, Day Camps, Movies

This chapter may seem overwhelming, but you can do this. You are not alone. You are called and equipped. "[You] can do all things through Christ who strengthens [you]" (Philippians 4:13).

Chapter 6

The Loyal Family
Serving on a Church Staff

For by grace you have been saved through faith,
and that not of yourselves; it is the gift of God, not
of works, lest anyone should boast. For we are His
workmanship, created in Christ Jesus for good
works, which God prepared beforehand that we
should walk in them.

—Ephesians 2:8–10

Serving on a church staff is a lot like being in a family. You do not get to choose the members, but you work with who you have. I once heard someone say he was amazed God could get any work done in such a corrupt environment. He was referring to the church. The comment saddend me but did not surprise me. I have served on several church staffs over the past thirty years, and I have to admit some have presented challenges.

We all have strengths and gifts, but we all have our imperfections too. It is important to remind yourself that church staffs are made up of imperfect people serving a perfect God in an imperfect world. Let me stress the word *imperfect*. Imperfection is necessary for us to truly understand grace and our need for God. It is important for us to embrace the people on our staffs with the same love, grace, respect, and loyalty we need and expect from them (Matt. 22:37–40; Luke 6:31). Remember, we are all a part of the body of Christ and no part is more important than another. Sometimes church staffs can be quite dysfunctional. We are all broken people who need the grace of God.

Helpful Hint

Remember church staffs are made up of imperfect people serving a perfect God in an imperfect world.

It is a challenge for some to understand that the church must function like a business, but remain a spiritual refuge. The church must have personnel policies, budgets, job descriptions, evaluations, performance expectations, and scheduled work hours. The church is also not immune to computer problems, space issues, time constraints, and personality clashes. The larger the staff, the more issues a church can experience. It is important to remember the power of prayer and grace. I currently serve on staff at the First United Methodist Church in Lakeland, Florida. There are more than one hundred people on the church's payroll, so you would think there would be constant staff issues and conflicts. This is not the case. We occasionally face difficult issues, but we have several policies and procedures in place to help us work through issues with love, grace, respect, and loyalty.

Building a Loving, Grace-filled, Respectful, and Loyal Family

At my current church, the first step to building a loving staff-family is how we go about selecting new staff members. It all begins in the hiring process. First UMC Lakeland looks for three Cs in hiring: competence, commitment, and chemistry. Regardless of your church or denomination, these three Cs can form the basis of any interview process.

- Competence: Can the person perform the duties required for the job? Can that candidate do them well? Does the person take pride in his or her job?
- Commitment: Is the person committed to Christ? Is the candidate committed to the mission of the church?
- Chemistry: Will the person be able to establish a working relationship with the current staff and congregation? Will that person be happy at the church, and will she or he work and play well with others?

Once we determine a job applicant has the three Cs, he or she is asked to review our staff behavioral covenant before deciding if he or she wishes to be in ministry with us. Each year our current church staff writes the behavioral covenant and states how we each plan to work together as a staff. Each staff member signs the covenant as a statement showing his or her willingness to adhere to the covenant.

You may want to establish your own staff behavioral contract. Here are a few suggestions to help you get started.

- Embrace your staff with love, grace, respect, and loyalty.
- Give love, grace, respect, and loyalty in return.
- Pray for every member of your staff.
- Be on time to meetings and come prepared.
- Dress professionally. (Youth ministers are known to have the most difficulty with this one.)
- Do not text or take phone calls during meetings. It is important to let the leader of the meeting know if you are expecting a call and that you may need to step out to take a call.
- If you have negative feedback for another staff member, give it to her or him in private.
- Be on time to work and keep regular office hours. If you have an administrative assistant, always let that person know your schedule.

- If you are fortunate enough to have an administrative assistant and a maintenance staff, treat them *well*. They are imperative to your ministry.
- Encourage everyone in their ministry areas.
- Act on and presume the best motives.
- Listen to others.
- Work to understand one another's responsibilities and time constraints.
- Honor your pastor(s) as servants called by God.
- Affirm one another's gifts.
- Take responsibility for your actions.
- Seek and offer forgiveness.
- Honor confidentiality/avoid gossip.
- Honor the personal time of staff members. Try not to call, text, or e-mail them on their days off or evenings.
- Practice self-care.
- Take your days off, and take time for spiritual growth.

Developing your own covenant in your church will help your staff become a loyal family. Remember to view successful ministry as God working *through* you. Continue to be an open vessel, and keep God in control. This will help you avoid the "proud cloud" as I like to call it. The "proud cloud" is the phrase I use to describe the surroundings of a person who feels his or her ministry area, or even the entire church, could not continue if that person was not there. It is a sense of entitlement. People who are surrounded by the "proud cloud" feel they work harder or have more talent than anyone else on their staff or ministry team. This cloud usually appears after a person has been successful in ministry for a few years, or has just completed seminary or divinity school. Remember, no ministry program can be successful with you alone, and the overall ministry of God's church is your ultimate goal. There is no room for the "proud cloud."

Warning!

This cloud contains dangerous levels of arrogance and piety that can harm self and others. This should not be present in a church setting. It is especially dangerous to church staffs. The cloud cannot be used by people who are filled with grace or who give or receive grace. Known side effects of the cloud are alienation of peers, resentment, self-fulfillment over ministry, and, in extreme cases, loss of appetite for spiritual food or loss of job.

Chapter 7

Denomination or Nondenominational?
That Is the Question

Then he said, "The God of our fathers has chosen
you that you should know His will, and see the Just
One, and hear the voice of His mouth."
                                        —Acts 22:14

Many believe that mainstream denominations are
the same and that differences between a denominational church and a nondenominational church are
insignificant. You may believe that differences are so
insignificant that it is easy to change denominations or
leave a denomination as a youth minister. If you are considering a change, reflect upon your choice prayerfully
and thoughtfully. Do your homework. It is not quite as
easy as you would think.

Understanding Other Denominations and Churches

I grew up as a Baptist. I went on to attend Presbyterian
and Baptist colleges. I have happily served as a staff member for three different denominations. Some transitions

were easier than others. As a college student it was easy for me not to notice the differences as much, but when I became a full-time staff member the challenges were more numerous and difficult to navigate. One denomination or church is no better than another. Each of God's churches has wonderful ministries that will enrich your life. Every church I served blessed and taught me in some way despite some very significant differences.

Each denomination or nondenominational church has its own vocabulary that you will need to learn. My first experience with the learning curve took place at the First United Methodist Church of Hendersonville, North Carolina. After having been in ministry for more than seven years in the Baptist denomination, I decided that I wanted to move back to my hometown. A friend in the chaplaincy department at the local hospital found out about an opening for a youth director at a United Methodist church and told me it was a wonderful church with wonderful ministries throughout the community. If I applied for the job, I knew I would need to do some research. I met with a United Methodist minister in the town where I then served to discuss theological differences and similarities. After talking with the pastor, I felt comfortable with the change. I applied and was granted an interview. The interview focused on personality, qualifications, and ability to relate to teenagers. It was a wonderful interview. I was elated to receive the job offer and I was thrilled to accept.

The challenges came my first week on the job. I was in a meeting with my adult council when the members posed this question: "What do you have planned for UMYF?" I was totally thrown by the question. I had no idea what UMYF was. I sat in silence trying to think what UMYF could possibly be an acronym for. Then someone asked, "What do you have planned for Sunday-night youth?" They helpfully explained that UMYF was an acronym for United Methodist Youth Fellowship, which at the time was the name for the Sunday-night youth ministries of The United Methodist Church. Oh, I had a plan; I just did not know what I had a plan for. I was fortunate to be a part of a council who was not only willing to laugh about the misunderstanding but to offer forgiveness. I was blessed by the guidance they provided me regarding United Methodist beliefs and policies.

I wish this had been my only mistake in my newfound denominational home, but I went on to experience many more "learning opportunities." In my first few months as part of The United Methodist Church I learned about the social principles, *The Discipline*, bishops, prevenient grace, infant baptism, administrative board, Council on Ministries, pledging, Staff-Parish Relations Committees, YSF (Youth Service Fund), UMCOR (United Methodist

Committee on Relief), and district superintendents. There are just a few examples of the new vocabulary I had to learn and use.

Helpful Hint

Research the theology and the structure of any church you consider applying to for a youth ministry position.

I will be eternally grateful to Leslie Merrill, the director of Christian education, Reverend Bud Lawing, the associate pastor, and a wonderful youth council who patiently taught me the policies and procedures in The United Methodist Church. For that I will always be grateful. Since my new church was part of a denomination, it was critical that I become familiar with the curriculum and vacation Bible school material from The United Methodist Church. The adult council who planned and implemented all youth events was instrumental in helping me gain a clear understanding of my new denomination and its resources. Regardless of whether the church you serve is part of a denomination or is nondenominational, you will need to work with staff and member committees to select material to meet your church's needs.

Every church you serve will provide opportunities to learn and grow in your faith and knowledge. Be grateful for the blessings you receive and the lessons you learn from every person you serve. The key to your happy transition is the willingness of the people you serve to help you learn and grow. If you plan on changing denominations you must first share core theological beliefs with the denomination or nondenominational church you are considering. Review your current pension plan because it will most likely not transfer. You may want to consult with an accountant. Be prepared for a change in your status. No, I am not talking about your Facebook status. You may now be a leader within your current denomination. Maybe you have written curriculum, been a speaker at events, or served on denominational committees. These things do not carry over. You will most likely have to reestablish yourself in these areas.

Helpful Hint

If you are changing denominations, consult an accountant. Most likely your pension plan is nontransferable.

It is also important to ask during the interview process if you could have a mentor to help you understand the organizational differences as well as the theological differences. Ask the interviewer to help you find the right person in the congregation to help mentor you and help you on your journey. I have included a list of well-known publishing companies for various denominations and nondenominational churches.

Helpful Hint

Ask for a mentor to help you through your transition into your new church position.

Denominational and Nondenominational Publishing Companies

Assemblies of God
Gospel Publishing House

Baptist

American Baptist Churches, USA
Judson Press

Baptist Missionary Association of America
Baptist Publishing House

Southern Baptist Convention
Broadman & Holman Publishing
Lifeway Christian Resources

Unaffiliated
Smyth & Helwys

Christian Church (Disciples of Christ)
Christian Board of Publication

Christian Reformed Church
CRC Publications

Church of God
Warner Press

Episcopal Church
Church Publishing
Cowley Publications
Forward Movement
Leader Resources

Lutheran
Evangelical Lutheran Church in America
Augsburg Fortress Publishers

The Lutheran Church-Missouri Synod
Concordia Publishing House

Mennonite Church
Faith and Life Press
Herald Press

Nazarene
   Beacon Hill Press

Nondenominational/Mainstream Christian
   Group Publishing
   Thomas Nelson Publishing
   Youth Specialties

Presbyterian Church
   Cumberland Presbyterian Church
   Board of Christian Education

   Presbyterian Church in America
   Great Commission Publications

   Presbyterian Church (U.S.A.)
   Bridge Resources
   Curriculum Publishing
   Presbyterian Publishing House
   Witherspoon Press

United Church of Christ
   Pilgrim Press
   United Church Press

United Methodist Church
   Abingdon Press
   Cokesbury
   Upper Room

Chapter 8

The 411 on Avoiding 911
Information on Youth Protection

By this we know that we love the children of God,
when we love God and keep His commandments.
—1 John 5:2

A great deal of this manual is devoted to keeping youth safe in your church. It is a sad reality that much time and energy must be devoted to this task. If you choose to read any one chapter of this manual, choose this chapter.

The Florida United Methodist Conference offers a child/youth protection policy template for United Methodist churches in Florida. It includes requirements and guidelines for churches to use in creating their own policies. It is important for all churches to implement policies and adopt procedures to protect children/youth and recognize that our Christian faith calls us to offer both hospitality and protection. The social principles of The United Methodist Church state that "children must be protected from economic, physical, and sexual exploitation and abuse" (*The Book of Resolutions of The United Methodist Church*, 2008, §162C). Tragically, churches have not always been safe places for children and youth. Child sexual abuse and exploitation occur in churches both large and small, urban and rural. The problem cuts across all economic, cultural, and racial lines. God calls us to make our churches safe places, protecting children and other vulnerable persons from abuse.

It is important that every church has child/youth protection policies and procedures in place to keep children/youth safe and procedures in place for reporting abuse. Carefully selecting staff/volunteers and properly supervising them is the key to child/youth safety. More injuries, legal claims, and lawsuits emanate from improper supervision than from any other reason, including using unsafe facilities. Focus on supervision.

How to Develop a Protection Policy

Check with your denomination headquarters to see if there is a template or policy to use as a guide. Decide who will write the policy and how it will be adopted. This individual or group could be an elder, board deacon, board personnel committee, Staff-Parish Relations Committee, church council, administrative council, pastor, or staff committee. It will be helpful to have an attorney and childcare advocate involved.

> Then I will give them one heart and one way, that they
> may fear Me forever, for the good of them and their
> children after them.
>
> —Jeremiah 32:39

Protection Policy Guidelines

You can have a combined policy for children and youth, if necessary. Both examples are included to help you get started. If your church decides to have a combined policy, make sure you include the children's minister when developing your plan. Make sure to have addenda for policies that might be children or youth ministry specific.

Definitions

Begin by establishing definitions for what ages your church considers children and what ages are considered youth. Define "paid staff person," "adult volunteer," "screened adult volunteer," and "youth helper." Also, define child/youth abuse in its many forms.

PAID STAFF PERSON. A paid staff person would be defined as someone your congregation has hired and pays through the church's budget. In the Florida Conference of The United Methodist Church, a paid staff person is someone paid by the church and overseen by a Staff-Parish Relations Committee.

ADULT VOLUNTEER. Specify a minimum age for adult volunteers. Does your church want this set at eighteen, twenty-one, or some other age? In the case of an adult volunteer for youth events, is the person old enough for the youth in your church to perceive the individual as an authority figure? If the person grew up in the youth group and just graduated from high school, this might be a problem. Also specify if a person must be a church member in order to volunteer. Will you allow members and nonmembers to volunteer? If you allow nonmembers, how long should she or he be in attendance before being allowed to volunteer? If she or he is a member, do you require a minimum membership time before she or he can volunteer?

SCREENED ADULT VOLUNTEER. Screened adult volunteers are people for whom you have checked references and conducted background screenings. It is up to your church to decide if you do national or state background screenings as well as national sex offender database searches. You will find resources in the back of this manual to help you decide if your church should conduct one or all of these types of screenings.

YOUTH HELPER. A youth helper is someone below the age of eighteen assisting with child or youth activities. He or she can assist with activities but should not be considered an adult volunteer and should also be supervised.

PHYSICAL ABUSE. Physical abuse could be defined as violent, non-accidental contact that results in injury. This includes, but is not limited to, striking, biting, or shaking. Injuries include bruises, fractures, cuts, and burns.

SEXUAL ABUSE. Sexual abuse could be defined as any form of sexual activity with a child/youth, whether at the church, at a home, or in any other setting. The abuser may be an adult, an adolescent, or another minor.

EMOTIONAL ABUSE. You could define emotional abuse as a pattern of intentional conduct that crushes a child's/youth's spirit or attacks his or her self-worth through rejection, threats, terror, isolation, or belittlement.

Warning!

Background checks are only as good as the police agencies reporting. (Not all jurisdictions are computer literate.) A background check is only one layer of a comprehensive review process.

Screening and Selecting Church Staff and Adult Volunteers

Decide how you will screen adult volunteers. Remember, you must receive a written authorization from the potential staff member or volunteer to run a background screening on him or her. Here are five things to think about when creating a screening plan:

1. Will you do a state screening, a national screening, or both?

2. Will you ask for and check references?

3. Will you have the potential volunteer sign a conduct policy?

4. Will you conduct interviews?

5. Will you require drug screening for adult staff, volunteers, or both?

Warning!

Please note not all counties in your state may report abuse cases to the state, so you may also need to do a separate screening for your county.

Ongoing Education of a Person Who Works with Children, Youth, or Both

Decide how often you will require training of staff and volunteers. Training should be required for all paid staff and for adult volunteers who work consistently with children, youth, or both.

Here is a list of training suggestions:

- Define and recognize child abuse.
- Review church policy and procedures on child abuse and the reasons for having them.
- Express the need to maintain a positive classroom environment, including appropriate discipline, and age-level characteristics.
- Outline appropriate behaviors for teachers and leaders of child/youth events.
- Go over responsibilities and procedures for reporting abuse.
- Define appropriate interpersonal boundaries.

Supervising Children and Youth

There are a few general rules you will need to establish, along with age-specific rules. Here are three suggested issues for which you should have established policies.

1. Decide what activities will require screened adults.

2. Will you require each classroom used for children to have windows/half doors?

3. Will there be a "two-person rule" (two people present in each classroom setting)?

For each age group you should establish specific rules about supervising classroom activities.

1. Crib/Toddler to Grade 2
   - What is the child-to-adult ratio?
   - Establish a check-in/checkout procedure.
   - Establish diaper changing and bathroom policies.

2. Grades 3–5
   - How many screened adults will be required in classrooms or in off-site activities?
   - Establish child-to-adult ratios and bathroom policies.
   - Establish check-in/checkout procedures.

3. Grades 6–12
   - How many screened adults will be required in classrooms or in off-site activities?
   - Establish child-to-adult ratios and bathroom policies.
   - Establish check-in/checkout procedures.

OPEN-DOOR POLICY. Will parents, volunteers, or church staff be permitted, as reasonably necessary, to visit and observe all programs and classrooms at any time?

SUPERVISING NONCLASSROOM ACTIVITIES. It should be established that at least two screened adults will be present for all nonclassroom activities involving children, youth, or both. Any meeting held in an individual's home should be supervised by at least two adults who are not members of the same family. Any meeting taking place in an individual's home should be approved by the participating child's parent or guardian.

COUNSELING CHILDREN/YOUTH. If one-on-one counseling is advised for a child/youth and would be most effective on a one-on-one basis, an appropriate church paid staff person may meet individually with a child. Here are three things to consider when planning for one-on-one child counseling:

1. During one-on-one counseling, having open doors or windows is mandatory and should be part of your policy.

2. The church staff should determine that the counselor is qualified to address the person's needs effectively.

3. Decide if there should be a session limit and when and if referrals to a licensed professional should be made.

DRIVING POLICIES. Transporting children/youth is an important concern. Their safety can be at risk in a variety of ways. Here are some recommended requirements.

1. The designated adult leader must know the drivers.

2. Drivers of a church-owned vehicle must be of age in order to be included on the church's insurance policy.

3. A driver must have a valid driver's license. (A copy of the driver's license should be on file at the church.)

4. A driver and passengers should be required to use seat belts.

5. A driver should be advised of a designated route and should not deviate from it unless there are detours.

6. A designated staff member should obtain motor vehicle driving records for all drivers.

7. Drivers should be accompanied by at least one other adult.

8. Drivers should receive training for the church-owned vehicle being operated.

9. Drivers should not use cell phones unless communicating with other drivers on the same

trip. Texting is never acceptable while driving. Hands-free cell phone use or pulling the car over are preferable ways to handle talking to other drivers on the same trip. Many states now have laws against cell phone use while driving.

10. When there is reason to believe it would not be safe for a youth to ride in a vehicle driven by another youth, the adults responsible should intervene and take reasonable steps to make alternative arrangements for all concerned. Laws regarding teenage drivers vary from state to state. Make sure your policies are in accordance with your state's regulations.

Helpful Hint

Transporting children or youth in non-church-owned vehicles (personal vehicles) should be discouraged, if possible. It is difficult to verify if the vehicle is safe and in proper working order. Volunteer drivers driving their own vehicles sometimes do not want to submit to a Moving Violations Report (MVR). Church insurance policies may not cover personal vehicles. You must check your church's policy.

Trip and Retreat Supervision

Retreat and trip settings can call for different child/youth protection requirements, depending on the circumstances. It is important to have policies in place to cover various settings and plans. There should be both requirements and guidelines.

Suggested Requirements

There should be at least two screened adults present for all trips, retreats, and other events where children/youth stay overnight at, or away from, the church campus.

There should be at least one screened adult for each gender present at overnight events where there are opposite genders present. If the event has just one gender present, there must be two screened adults of the same gender as the children/youth.

Permission forms that include permission from parents to be taken off the church campus as well as permission for emergency care should be in the leader's possession at all times.

Suggested Guidelines

In a hotel-type setting, rooms should be assigned as follows:

1. Separate rooms for adults and children/youth should be assigned with at least two children/youth per room.

2. Assignments should be made so that an adult room is between two children/youth rooms.

3. Adults should make random hall monitoring trips and room checks at night. Room checks should be conducted by two adults of the same gender as those being checked.

4. A hotel should be selected where rooms open to the interior of the building (rooms do not open to the outside).

5. In home stay settings, extreme care should be given to ensure youth are placed in a home with youth and children of the same gender. Single-parent housing should be avoided. Youth should be assigned as follows:

   - two youth (same gender);
   - one youth, one adult (same gender).

Separate rooms should be provided for each person staying in someone's home.

PARTICIPATION COVENANT. Will you require a participation covenant to be signed by volunteers, staff, or both? A participation covenant is a statement signed by participants in your ministry (paid or volunteer) that states participants have read the rules set forth by the church and will abide by them.

RESPONDING TO ALLEGATIONS OF CHILD ABUSE. Everyone in the church has a moral responsibility and legal duty to report suspected abuse whenever it comes to their attention, regardless of where abuse takes place. Reporting abuse is a way of ministering to the needs of those crying out for help.

Helpful Hint

Establish a policy for reporting abuse! Check with local authorities and state child protection agencies regarding reporting requirements. Specifically note the requirements in your policy. Cite them specifically, and include child-abuse hotline phone numbers in the policy.

Implementation

Meet with your pastor and decide who will be in charge of implementing the child and youth protection policies and procedures. Implementation of your policies usually happens more efficiently if a committee is assigned this task. The committee's responsibility will be to design the policies, conduct training on them, and ensure their effectiveness.

Sample Forms

The next several pages consist of sample forms that may be used as a guide to help you establish your own policies. Many states have different reporting, recording, and screening procedures. Please make sure the forms you use at your church are approved by your church's attorney or appropriate committees.

Sample Participation Covenant Statement

Participation Covenant

The congregation of _____
Church is committed to providing a safe and secure
environment for all children, youth, and volunteers
who participate in ministries and activities spon-
sored by the church. The following policy statement
reflects our congregation's commitment to preserv-
ing the church as a holy place of safety and protection for all who would enter, and as a place in which
all people can experience the love of God through
relationships with others.

No adult who has been convicted of child abuse
(either sexual abuse or physical abuse) should work
with children or youth in any church-sponsored
activity. Emotional abusers should also be barred
from working with children. All adults involved
with children or youth of our church must have
been active participants of the congregation for
at least six months before beginning a volunteer
assignment. All adults involved with children and
youth of our church shall observe the child protection policy at all times.

All adults involved with children and youth of
our church shall attend regular training and educational events provided by the church to keep
volunteers informed of church policies and laws
regarding child abuse.

All adults involved with children and youth of our church shall immediately report to their supervisors any behavior that seems abusive or inappropriate.

Please answer the following question:

Do you agree to observe and abide by all church policies regarding working in ministries with children and youth? ___ Yes ___ No

I have read this participation covenant, and I agree to observe and abide by the policies set forth above.

_____

Signature of applicant: _____

Date: _____

I have read the child protection policies and agree to abide by all policies.

_____

Signature of applicant: _____

Date: _____

Print full name: _____

Sample Parental Consent and Medical Authorization

Please check with your church's attorney before using this form to make sure it meets the standards set by your state.

(Church name and address)

Parental Consent and Medical Authorization

Name of child/youth: _____

Grade: _____ Age: _____

Address: _____

Apt. #: _____ City: _____ Zip Code:_____

Daytime phone number: _____

Cell phone number(s):_____

As the parent (or legal guardian) of:

_____ ,

(Child's/youth's name)

I understand that my child/youth will be participating in a number of activities for the calendar year _____, which carry with them a certain degree of risk. Some of the activities are swimming, boating, hiking, camping, field trips, sports, and other activities that the church may offer. I consent for my child to participate in these activities.

Please indicate any restrictions on your child's/youth's activities:

_____ I represent that my child/youth is physically fit and has the necessary skills to safely participate in these activities.

_____ I represent that my child/youth has restrictions on the following particular activities:

_____.

_____

_____ I also understand and give consent for my child to travel to and from these events in transportation provided by volunteer drivers.

Medical Treatment Authorization

It is my understanding that the church will attempt to notify me in case of a medical emergency involving my child/youth. If the church cannot find me, then I authorize the church to hire a doctor or health-care professional, and I give my permission to the doctor or other health-care professional to provide the medical services he or she may deem necessary. I will pay for any medical expenses so incurred.

I will notify the church if I feel there are any health considerations that would prevent my child's/youth's participation in any of the activities listed above.

Allergies or other health considerations: ____

_____

Insurance company: _____

Policy/Group #: _____

Signature of parent or guardian: _____

Date: _____

Sample Child/Youth Protection Incident Form

Child/Youth Protection Incident Report Form

Reason for the report: _____

Date of incident: _____ Time: _____

Place of incident: _____

Name of reporter: _____

Title: _____

Name(s) of child(ren)/youth: _____

Age(s): _____

Briefly describe what happened:

_____

_____

_____

_____

Were there any witnesses? ____ Yes ____ No

If yes, list: _____

_____

What action did you take?

_____

_____

Has the incident been resolved? ____ Yes ____ No

Explain:

_____

_____

_____

Have the following people been notified?

Pastor _____   Bishop's Office _____

Parent _____   Police _____

Deacon/SPRC Chair ____   Sheriff _____

District Supervisor ____

Signature of reporter: _____ Date: _____

Report submitted to: _____

Sample Emergency Contact

Emergency Contact Information

Pastor(s): _____

Home phone number: _____

Cell phone number(s): _____

Chairperson(s) of SPRC: _____

Home phone number: _____

Cell phone number(s): _____

Director of children's ministries: _____

Home phone number: _____

Cell phone number(s): _____

Director of youth ministries: _____

Home phone number: _____

Cell phone number(s): _____

State or district denomination leader: ____

Church administrator: _____

Home phone number: _____

Cell phone number(s): _____

(Add any additional contact information for your church's Personnel Committee, Human Resource Committee, etc.)

City police department: _____

County sheriff's department: _____

State abuse hotline: _____

(You may want to list the contact information for your state's denominational office.)

Church attorney: _____

Sample Reference Check

Reference Check (by phone or by mail)

Applicant name: _____

Reference name: _____

Phone number: _____

Address: _____

City: _____ Zip Code: _____

What is your relationship to the applicant? _____

How long have you known the applicant? _____

How well do you know the applicant? _____

How would you describe the applicant? _____

_____

How would you describe the applicant's ability to relate
to children/youth? _____

_____

_____

How would you describe the applicant's leadership
abilities? _____

_____

How would you describe the applicant's ability to relate
to adults? _____

_____

How would you feel about having the applicant as a
volunteer worker with your child or youth?

_____

_____

Do you know of any reason whatsoever that this person should *not* work with children?

_____

If yes, please explain: _____

_____

_____

Do you have any knowledge that the applicant has ever been charged with or convicted of a crime? _____

If so, please describe: _____

_____

Please list the names of other people you feel it would be beneficial for us to contact before making a decision on whether or not the applicant should work with children or youth and please indicate a means of contacting them.

_____

_____

Please list any other comments you would like to make:

_____

_____

Reference inquiry completed by:

_____   _____
            Signature   Date

You may return this form to _____

(Add church name and specific person to receive reference.)

Sample Authorization and Request for Criminal Records Check

Authorization and Request for Criminal Records Check

I, _____, HEREBY AUTHORIZE the (*Name of the Church*) to request any local, state, or federal law enforcement department or agency to release information regarding any record of any investigations, charges, or convictions contained in its files, or in any criminal file maintained on me, whether said file is a local, state, or national file, and including but not limited to accusations and convictions for crimes committed, against minors, to the fullest extent permitted by local, state, and federal law. I release any and all law enforcement departments, agencies, and their employees from all liability that may result from any such disclosure made in response to this request. I also give my permission for this information to be shared with those persons who will participate in making decisions with respect to my application.

You are authorized to rely upon a photocopy or faxed copy of this document.

Signature of applicant: _____

Date: _____

Print full name:_____

Print all other names that have been used by applicant (if any):

_____

Date of birth: _____ Place of birth: _____

Social Security number: _____

Driver's license number: _____

State in which the license was issued: _____

License expiration date: _____

Request sent to: _____

Name: _____

Address: _____

Phone number: _____

- You may need to make a photocopy of the applicant's driver's license. Some state background search organizations ask for race, and you may not ask one's race on the application form.
- Always keep these documents in a locked file cabinet since they include personal information.
- The form should be shredded when no longer needed.

Chapter 9

Oh, the Things You Will Know about the Places You Go
Overnight Trips and Retreats

I am not a huge "rule" person and I usually do not speak in absolutes, but this chapter is the exception.

There are absolutely some rules in planning trips and retreats you should never overlook. Yep, I said it. So listen up!

1. Trips and retreats must have a purpose and require planning. You may call it a "Mystery Trip," but you do not want surprises on a trip.

2. Always have adequate supervision. See chapter 8 for guidelines.

Whenever I speak with a former youth about their youth group memories, she or he always talks about a retreat, mystery trip, or mission trip. Trips are essential in youth ministry because they take youth away from their comfort zones and daily distractions. Youth trips help youth bond as a group and experience some independence from their parents. This is a very important part of spiritual and developmental growth.

Helpful Hint

The key to a successful trip is the planning. If everything is well planned you will have time to focus on relationship building rather than trip details while on the trip.

Retreat

One definition of the word *retreat* is to "withdraw from enemy forces as a result of their superior power." Teens have always been influenced by their surroundings, but today, more than ever, their surroundings can feel like an enemy force with superior powers. Many times it actually is filled with "enemies." Teens feel over-committed, overstimulated, and overwhelmed. When you use the word *retreat* in the form of a verb you understand the need for youth ministry retreats. Youth need to retreat. Thanks to social media and texting, many youth feel like they are in a crowd even when they are alone. Retreats offer the ideal setting for teaching youth how to have a quiet time with God or a daily devotion. Many teens may know how to pray but not know how or when God answers their prayers because they have never thought to take the time to listen. Retreats should be different from trips. Retreats should offer youth times of rest and reflection as well as activities. Retreat destinations such as the beach or mountains can be wonderful outreach tools. Youth love traveling to new places and trying activities that are not common to their area. Encourage youth to invite friends and work to provide fund-raising opportunities and/or sponsorship to any youth in need.

Here is a retreat/trip worksheet and some examples of retreat schedules to help you plan. These were actual retreat schedules used with real youth.

Trip/Retreat Worksheet

Destination _____

Housing _____ Cost? _____

Meals _____ Cost? _____

Mode of transportation _____

Approximate mileage? _____ Total cost? _____

Transportation rental cost _____

Supplies needed _____ Cost? _____

_____

_____

_____

_____

_____

_____

Number of adult leaders needed _____

Are adult leaders expected to pay their way?

Yes ____ No ____

Are adult leader costs included in the youth budget?

Yes ____ No ____

Will it be added to the cost per participant?

Yes ____ No ____

Is fund-raising an option for this event? Yes ____ No ____

How much will be provided from fund-raiser? ____

Are there scholarships/sponsorships available for youth who have need?

Yes ____ No ____ Amount? _____

Who will collect payments? _____

Will you require a deposit? Yes ____ No ____

How much? _____

What are payment deadlines? _____

Registration deadline? _____

Will you offer refunds if a youth cannot attend?

Yes ____ No ____

Retreat Packet

Cover page (include name of retreat, date, destination, and church name and address)

- Page 1—List of adults and youth attending (list adults' cell phone numbers)
- Page 2—Schedule(s)
- Page 3—Behavior covenant/Behavior guidelines or expectations

---

Behavior Covenant

Youth attending should develop their own covenant of behavior that everyone signs. Make a copy for each participant and include in each packet.

Sample Behavior Covenant

1. Be on time.
2. Respect one another's belongings.
3. No alcohol or non-personally prescribed drugs allowed.
4. No smoking.
5. Be kind to one another.
6. Stay in designated areas (boys with boys, girls with girls).
7. No purple! (That is, no mixing of pink and blue; known as public displays of affection.)
8. Respect property.

Ministry Tips

- The number of participants may be determined by housing, transportation, or supervision limits.
- If you are using church transportation, it is important to have vehicles checked at least two weeks prior to the trip in case repairs are needed.
- Make sure all drivers have been cleared to drive church vehicles or that drivers have adequate insurance to transport youth in their own vehicles. Check to see if your church's insurance has an age requirement for drivers. If you plan on renting vehicles, most rental companies require drivers to be at least twenty-five.
- Check your youth protection guidelines to see if you must have two adults per vehicle.
- Decide on the route.

Sample Ski Retreat Schedule

Friday

4:00 PM	**SHARP!** Leave church parking lot
5:00 PM	Stop at Wendy's in Old Fort
6:00 PM	Arrive at cabin and unpack
6:30–10:30 PM	Ski
11:00 PM	Arrive back at the cabin
11:30 PM	Devotions
12:00 Midnight	**LIGHTS OUT!**

Saturday

7:00 AM	**Rise and Shine!**
7:30 AM	Devotions
8:00 AM	Breakfast
9:00 AM	Ski
4:30 PM	Return ski equipment
5:30 PM	Arrive at cabin
7:00 PM	Dinner
8:30 PM	Bible study and worship
10:00 PM	Free time
11:30 PM	**LIGHTS OUT!**

Sunday

7:00 AM	**Rise and Shine!**
7:30 AM	Clean up
8:00 AM	Leave cabin and have breakfast
12:00 noon	Arrive home

Sample Beach Retreat Schedule

Sunday

3:00–4:00 PM	Arrive and settle in
4:00–5:00 PM	Gather supplies
5:00–6:00 PM	Free time
6:00–7:00 PM	Dinner and clean up
7:00–7:30 PM	Small-group time
7:30–8:00 PM	Large-group time
8:00–9:00 PM	Worship
9:00–11:00 PM	Free time
11:00–11:30 PM	In rooms
11:30 PM	**LIGHTS OUT!**

Monday–Friday

8:30 AM	**RISE AND SHINE!**
9:00 AM	Breakfast
9:30–9:45 AM	Clean up
9:45–10:00 AM	Quiet time
10:00–11:00 AM	Morning fun
11:00 AM–Noon	Two gather
Noon–1:00 PM	Lunch and clean up
1:00–5:00 PM	Beach/Free time
5:00–6:00 PM	Worship team
6:00–7:00 PM	Dinner and clean up
7:00–7:30 PM	Group time
7:30–8:00 PM	Large-group time
8:00–8:15 PM	Break
8:15–9:00 PM	Worship
9:00–11:00 PM	Free time
11:00–11:30 PM	Get ready for bed
11:30 PM	**LIGHTS OUT!**

Saturday

8:00 AM	**Rise and shine!**
8:30 AM	Breakfast
8:30–9:30 AM	Clean up and pack
9:30–10:00 AM	Reflections
10:00 AM	Head home

Helpful Tips

- Work to stay true to departure and arrival times. It shows you respect others' time. It is great to have an "on-call" parent who has a list of all phone numbers for parents who have children participating on any trip or retreat, so he or she can call or text the other parents if you are running late or arriving early. Parents become worried if they are sitting in a parking lot waiting.

- If cliques are a challenge in your youth group, you may wish to try a ski retreat. I have found that youth ski or snowboard in groups according to skill level more than their usual peer group.

- It is okay to have down time at a retreat. Many youth today do not know how to rest, relax, and just be with God. Teach them to have a quiet time each day reading their Bibles and praying. Most of all, teach them that listening is a part of prayer.

- High school retreats in July are great ways to send your graduated seniors off to college. You can end your retreat with a "College Survival Kit" packed with encouraging notes from the adults and students in the youth group, as well as parents and pastors.

- A retreat may not be the first event to which you want to invite new sixth or seventh graders. Many parents may not be familiar enough with the group and leaders to be comfortable with their children being away. Making a retreat the first event for sixth or seventh graders to participate in can easily divide the group before you begin. Sometimes you may have to win the parents' respect and confidence before they will allow their kids to go on overnight trips. This is not an insult to you or your ministry. I did not understand this until I was a parent.

- Find a company that specializes in organizing group ski packages or other group travel. A good company that will pay attention to the details

> for you can make your trip go more smoothly. A good example is CTI Group Adventures in Asheville, North Carolina, which does an excellent job organizing group ski packages.

Even Jesus felt the need to get away from the crowds to pray and rest. "So He Himself often withdrew into the wilderness and prayed" (Luke 5:16).

Mission Trips

I could write an entire book of mission trip stories alone. If I did, it would have to have an MT-13 rating. This rating would recommend that the book only be read by those who have been on at least thirteen mission trips before reading one page. The book would include:

Brief Nudity

One certain youth minister I know quite well unrolled toilet paper only to find two live twelve-inch centipedes in her lap while she sat on a particular throne. She quickly jumped up, screamed, and ran out of the room. The rest of this story has been told many times by the youth leaders and the youth mission team of her church.

Violence

The same youth minister mentioned above learned a very important lesson about repairing a clogged sink. Do not, under any circumstances, have a conversation with youth and adults while lying on your back under a kitchen sink while unscrewing the pipe with a wrench. This youth minister experienced a mouth full of rotted lettuce and mangoes. As soon as the rotted food hit her mouth she raised up as quickly as possible only to hit her head on the bottom of the sink, which led to a huge bump that almost knocked her out. This youth minister is still quite bitter about how hard the youth and adults laughed at the experience.

Language

It is very important to be able to trust your adult leaders on a mission trip, especially if they are fluent in the native language where you are working. One very trusting youth minister I know received a quick Spanish lesson from one of her adult leaders. This adult leader taught her how to ask for a receipt for gas. The youth minister became quite frustrated when the gas station attendant kept repeating he did not have receipts. The youth minister knew she had to have a receipt and could not understand that any place of business would not give any type of receipt to customers. When she returned to the van, the adult leader, who was laughing as hard as anyone possibly could, revealed she had taught her to ask for a recipe, not a receipt. The youth minister did think this was quite clever and only wished she spoke another language so she could be as cool as this jokester.

The reason this book could only be read by youth ministers who have led at least thirteen mission trips is because a veteran youth minister would know those are not the real stories that make you go back year after year. The stories that make you go back year after year are the stories of lives being changed for the better because you were there.

The Shirts Off Their Backs

The senior high mission team from Indian River City United Methodist Church chose to go to Vieques, Puerto Rico, during the summer of 1998. They chose Vieques because of a job request. They were to lay the foundation for a hurricane shelter. Youth from Florida understand hurricanes and the need for safety. They also loved the beach and felt it was a perfect fit.

When we arrived in Vieques, the pastor invited our group to stay in his home with his family instead of the church. Reverend

Edgardo Ortiz, his wife, Vanessa, and four children arranged to sleep in one room, borrowed army cots from the nearby army base, and treated us like family. Thirty people living in one house for a week had all the makings of a reality show, but we had a wonderful experience. Living in such close proximity, we learned a lot about one another quite quickly. The youth were amazed by how hard Pastor Ortiz worked to meet the needs of his congregation. Pastor Ortiz was blind but had a vision for the church like no other. His wife and family were all partners in his ministry. It was a privilege to be a part of their family.

The youth were so touched by the family's gracious hospitality that they wanted to purchase gifts for the family. They asked the children if they could have anything, what would they wish for. The youth thought they knew the answers and had created a list that included a CD player, new clothes, toys, maybe a skateboard or bike. They were absolutely surprised when the children said they would like new towels and T-shirts like ours. Used T-shirts and towels did not even make the list. The group was humbled by the children's wishes and not only purchased new towels and washcloths but decided to decorate the entire bathroom and gave T-shirts to the two teens and two small children. It was such a simple request. Their happiness was not based on material items but in the love of Jesus and family. They ministered to us! As we were riding in the ferry across the water to the main island we knew we had not only laid a firm foundation for the hurricane shelter but we had also built a friendship that could withstand much more than a Category 3 hurricane.

Less than three months later, Hurricane Georges hit Vieques with a vengeance. The youth in Titusville were watching the storm closely, knowing they had "family" there. The island suffered severe damage and the Ortiz family left with the clothes on their backs and eventually found safety and refuge in Alabama. They returned to Puerto Rico several years later to serve a church in Aguirre. Seven years after the mission trip to Vieques, I returned to Puerto Rico with a high school mission team from another church. To my amazement, I found one of the Ortiz children, now a teenager himself, wearing the T-shirt given to him by the group in Titusville. When I asked Vanessa about the T-shirt, she said when the family evacuated they knew they may never return and had to choose the clothes they wanted to leave in. The children chose the T-shirts. The shirts made them feel secure. Seven years later they were a perfect fit.

Not all mission trips will feel like a perfect fit, but I believe firmly that God is always in control, and the Holy Spirit is at work even when I do not get to see the results. My trip to Aguirre was a beautiful reminder of why we serve others. We are most like Jesus when we serve.

You do not have to plan your own mission trip or travel across an ocean to be like Jesus. There are many mission organizations that do a superb job discovering the needs in communities across the United States and other countries then matching the needs with the skill level provided by mission teams.

Some Resources for Mission Trips

Here is a list of the organizations I recommend and their contact information:

YouthWorks

- Web site: www.youthworks.com
- Ages: middle school, high school, middle and high school mix
- Location: rural, urban, city, American Indian, small town, international
- Types of projects and activities: making minor repairs, working with homeless people, conducting children's ministry, and more
- Structure: youth groups divided into small groups that include an adult leader from each participating church
- Things to keep in mind: Background searches are the responsibility of each church.
- Advantages: This mission is well organized, with a knowledgeable staff, and offers a variety of places to serve and a wide range of mission opportunities at an affordable price.

Appalachia Service Project

- Web site: www.asphome.org
- Ages: fourteen and up
- Location: twenty-seven rural communities in central Appalachia, which include parts of Kentucky, Virginia, West Virginia, and Tennessee

- Types of projects and activities: repairing roofs, building handicapped ramps, and performing a host of other improvements and repairs
- Structure: work teams divided into crews of seven, with two adults needed for every five youth
- Things to keep in mind: Sign up early, and do not miss the deadline!
- Advantages: Required advanced preparation is a great opportunity for your team to begin bonding, while learning about the communities they will serve. There is a good group application process, and this organization provides excellent opportunities to learn about the people and community your group will be serving.

TEAMeffort

- Web site: www.teameffort.org
- Ages: rising sixth grade to high school
- Location: TEAMeffort has camps throughout the United States, Puerto Rico, Bahamas, and Guatemala
- Types of projects and activities: repairing and renovating homes, building mission and ministry facilities, leading children's outreach

programs, working in homeless shelters, and responding to natural disasters

- Structure: Groups stay together on mission sites but larger groups may be divided.
- Things to keep in mind: If you plan on taking a chartered bus please let TEAMeffort know in advance so you can be placed where the bus can travel safely.
- Advantages: TEAMeffort is especially appropriate for middle school students because it has a great mix of work and free time.

ReCreation Experiences

- Web site: www.recreationexperiences.org
- Ages: middle school and above
- Location: western North Carolina
- Types of projects and activities: home repair for low-income and fixed-income families
- Structure: no minimum or maximum group size
- Things to keep in mind: This organization provides great experiences for youth and adults.
- Advantages: affordable

Teen Missions International

- Web site: www.teenmissions.org
- Ages: thirteen and up for mission teams

- Location: United States and abroad
- Types of projects and activities: Camps for children ages four and above prepare children and youth for the mission field. Mission teams work on building projects, lead camps, and work with children.
- Structure: groups placed in teams
- Things to keep in mind: All team members are asked to participate. You will be sleeping in tents.
- Advantages: team building

Group Workcamps

- Web site: www.groupworkcamps.com
- Ages: ten through eighteen
- Location: seventeen U.S. locations and Puerto Rico
- Types of projects and activities: home repair
- Structure: church groups are divided into small teams
- Things to keep in mind: Participants from a variety of churches will be placed on work crews. You may call ahead if you would like other arrangements.
- Advantages: This is one of the few organizations that offers opportunities for pre-teens to do community service.

Catholic HEART Workcamps
- Web site: www.heartworkcamp.com
- Ages: rising eighth graders and up
- Location: camps throughout the United States
- Types of projects and activities: renewing homes, doing yard work, and assisting with childcare
- Structure: groups of all sizes will be split into groups of seven with one adult
- Things to keep in mind: Each group requires one adult, age twenty-one or older, for every five youth. Some camps allow you to bring rising seventh graders and some camps allow only rising ninth graders and above.
- Advantages: team building, experiencing diversity

Reach Workcamps
- Web site: www.reachwc.org
- Ages: rising seventh graders and above
- Location: camps throughout the United States
- Types of projects and activities: home repairs
- Structure: groups divided into work crews
- Things to keep in mind: The group will stay in a local school for the week; the vehicles you bring for the week are the vehicles you will use to get to the worksites. Not all meals are provided.

- Advantages: Reach will pay for any gas used to transport crews to and from worksites.

Hassle-free Mission Trip Planning

TAKE TIME. Mission trip planning should begin six to nine months before the actual trip. Prayerfully consider where God is calling your mission team. Determine the age or grade level required to participate in the trip. If you plan on using a mission organization, it is especially important to be familiar with their age and grade requirements. Recruit leaders early and require them to attend training and pre-trip meetings with teens.

Helpful Hint

Make sure you know what the age and grade requirements are for any mission organization you use. Every organization has different policies.

CHOOSE LEADERS WISELY. Carefully choose adult leaders. Choose leaders who are passionate about their faith as well as have a love of teens. It is tempting to invite someone to be an adult leader on a mission trip because of their construction skills, music skills, and so forth, but the person also has to live with teens for a week. You can avoid a lot of frustration by choosing leaders who interact well with youth and who are not rigid about schedules or have the need to be young themselves.

Helpful Hint

Be flexible and choose leaders of like mind. Flexibility is one key to a successful mission trip because your time is not your own.

BE CLEAR ABOUT EXPECTATIONS! Do not underestimate the impact—both positive and negative—parents and grandparents can have on youth while everyone serves on a mission trip. It truly depends on the family. Do not dismiss anyone on the basis of age alone. I have led several mission trips with three generations from one family, and they were some of the most meaningful trips in all my years of ministry. Two of my all-time favorite and most effective adult leaders were well into their sixties. I have a wonderful memory of my friend Betty with her beautiful white hair pulled perfectly into a bun, standing on top of a house wearing her Habitat for Humanity T-shirt. That woman had more skill and energy than I will ever have. She is the only person I know who is probably asking God if she can build mansions in heaven rather than live in one. Do not underestimate the power of a cool grandma. Betty was the coolest and I am sure she holds the record for the most marriage proposals on one mission trip.

WATCH OUT FOR DEADLINES. Many mission organizations have an application process and strict deadlines. Most require deposits. Give yourself plenty of time to collect needed information and the money needed to secure your spot. Know the refund policy and communicate with parents.

ADVERTISE. Advertise your mission trip dates well in advance. It is helpful to parents and the church staff if your mission trips are the same week each summer. You may not always be able to schedule them this way, but you will find it makes it easier for participants and church staff when you can.

GO! Sleep on the floor, eat lots of peanut butter and jelly sandwiches, learn things you never thought you would, and share Jesus with the world. Why? Because the Bible says so!

Go therefore and make disciples of all nations, baptizing them in the name of the Father and of the Son and of the Holy Spirit, teaching them to observe all things that I have commanded you; and lo, I am with you always, even to the end of the age.

—Matthew 28:19–20

Chapter 10

The Life and Times of a Real Youth Minister

Have you ever wanted to be a caterer, travel agent, teacher, principal, counselor, referee, graphic designer, architect, custodian, bus driver, funeral director, coach, set designer, fund raiser, chaplain, preacher, pastor, circus leader, accountant, dance instructor, mover, event planner, babysitter, athlete, mom, or dad? Youth ministry offers you the opportunity to do them all. It is truly the only profession I can think of that calls for such a broad skill set.

Prepare yourself for huge myth busters. Here they are:

- There is no such thing as a typical day as a Youth Minister
- There is No Such Thing As a Typical Youth Minister

I racked my brain to think of one typical day in youth ministry. In over twenty years of ministry I cannot think of a single one. Now I can think of typical tasks that should be done daily such as answer the phone, return calls, answer emails, and scheduling. After all, youth ministry must be planned and planned well because the ministry happens in the interruptions. If you do not have your planning done then you will be ministering through chaos.

Youth ministry must happen in spite of chaos, but you want to avoid doing ministry through chaos. What is the difference? It is easy to fall into the mindset that ministry can just *happen*. Imagine this scenario. You can fly by the seat of your pants. Teens will come; you will hang out, play sports, music, and video games. Then they will open up a conversation about theology, and you will be able to answer all their questions. You will be the coolest in the youth group because you are the great Oracle (the keeper of the knowledge). You will wear cool clothes, have all the latest gadgets, and can play music and find really funny videos on You Tube and go on fun trips. Who would not want to do this? Here is a second scenario. What happens when God calls a middle aged woman who is not musical and can barely use a computer? Everyone knows that person could not succeed at youth ministry. Youth could not relate to a middle age woman. They can only relate to someone who looks and talks just like they do. They need someone different from their parents. They need a really cool adult. The youth/teens will be fooled into thinking this person is really just another teen and they will share all thoughts and secrets. The youth will beg this person to help them learn and grow spiritually.

The reality is that neither is true. Many youth ministers need to spend less time worrying about how cool they are and more time working on doing a good job. Youth ministry is a calling, and it is a job. It requires lots of hard work. Do not be fooled by thinking it is a perfect job where you can play and get paid. It is also a job that does not always look like a job, so people will have a difficult time understanding what you do and why you get paid. This is where planning, keeping set office hours, marketing your ministry, and communication with parents is imperative. I am not telling you not to have fun. Youth are fun and they want to have a good time. Balance is always they key.

The belief that age matters is such a sad misconception that it breaks my heart to write this. When God calls someone to youth ministry He equips them. Seriously, let's look at the people God called in the Bible. None of them would even pass our background screening let alone be able to offer a good reference. Anyone who knew them for over two years would know they weren't the best examples of Godly people. David, the Woman at the well, Esther, Moses, nope, none of them would have made the cut. Jesus Himself did not choose the twelve coolest people he could find.

Wait! Do not close the book and run! There is more, and it gets better I promise! Keep reading! Youth Ministers have the ability to change the world! Not many jobs can claim that but youth ministry certainly can.

What is the typical day of a life changer?

The typical day of a life changer begins with prayer. Spending time with God each day should be first on your list. I would love to say I have always done this but this is the first thing I use to cut from my day if it was going to be a long and busy day. I would try to tell myself the devotion in staff meeting or the Bible study I was working on was the same thing as reading my Bible and praying for the ministry and for others. It is never the same. Make time for God and listen to what God is telling you. Make time to listen.

I love the story of Samuel in 1 Samuel 3:1-10. Samuel was just a boy. His mother Hannah thought he was a gift from God and handed him over to the Priest. Many parents will just hand their youth over to you so you should be able to relate to this. Samuel, who was just a kid was given the job to guard the Ark of the Covenant. Now that is a big job! So there he is working for this really old Priest named Eli. Eli is asleep down the hall, while Samuel is on guard. He hears a voice. Frankly this would just freak me out, and I am an adult. Samuel ran to Eli to tell him about the voice. Now messages from the Lord were uncommon to say the least, and if God were to call me in an audible voice I do believe I would have bathroom issues. I do believe God has spoken to me, but I have not literally *heard* his voice. God usually communicated with me through Text Messages. No, I do not mean messages on my phone. I mean he uses his Text, the Bible, to send me messages. This reading in 1 Samuel certainly sent me a huge message that changed my ministry forever. The Lord was speaking and Samuel said the most amazing thing. He said "Speak Lord, For your servant hears."

Sometimes we forget when we are in the ministry that we are first and foremost servants of God. If we are His servants we must be ready to hear what He has to say before we even begin the day. When we miss that important message the day becomes about us or the tasks at hand. Even in the midst of the chaos of broken down church busses, unsigned permission forms, and computer viruses, we must be willing to say at the beginning of each day, "speak Lord, for your servant hears."

If we do not spend time reading God's text, we will never get the message. So many youth ministers are missing the message. It is about loving God, loving youth, and somehow helping them to understand that amazing, unconditional love and how it applies to their lives. The unconditional love of God is a life changer!

Now I have to admit when I have cleaned out busses, stayed up all night writing lesson plans, cleaned up vomit, and cleaned out closets to dispose of literature left from the 70s, I have not felt like a life changer. I did not hear God tell me to organize the youth room. These were very important tasks and needed to be done. Youth need and deserve a ministry that is well organized, safe, and relevant. They deserve trained leaders and strong theology. This is the foundation for change. The change occurs when they begin to hear the voice as well as feel the love. Lives are changed when a youth received their call to ministry.

Unforgettable Change

One of my most unforgettable moments was when a young man in eleventh grade ran to me during a "Capture the Flag" game and yelled, "I know what I am going to do with the rest of my life. I am going to be a youth minister." We ran to each other and hugged. It was amazing. He was so excited. He had been struggling and knew God was working in him but did not know what was happening. We were at a retreat and had spent much time in prayer. The youth were also asked to have a quiet time with God each day and just read scripture, be quiet, and listen. God spoke to him because he was willing to hear. There have been many times throughout my career that I have been privileged to witness God calling youth into the ministry. It is an amazing feeling. To date I know of at least fifty youth who have gone into various forms of ministry. I have always prayed the prayer "Lord, speak through me or in spite of me." Whatever the reason, I was glad to be a witness.

The Really Scared Youth Minister

Regardless of circumstances, hold on to the fact that God is in control. There have been times in the ministry when I knew God was present and in control. I absolutely knew it was not me. It happened when the situation called for much more than I could have provided. I always knew it. I asked, waited, and He came. Each time I called He came. Once He came to a restaurant on a Friday night as I sat in front of a middle school boy and his younger sister and told them God was going to get them through the next few months as their mother was packing to leave for a bone marrow transplant. I had no idea what type of cancer she had; I did not know the prognosis, and I did not know if she would ever come home. I just knew I loved them both, loved their family, and God was with us all. It was all I had to offer. The Holy Spirit had already been at work. They both looked at me and said "We will be fine." How in the world could they possibly know that? They were scared, sad, mad and tired but they knew they would be fine. They did not know the outcome but they had a very strong extended family, church family and a new youth minister who was willing to ride out any storm with them. They knew that "fine" did not mean their mom would be cured. "Fine" meant God was in control. Their faith ministered to me. That middle school boy is now the Pastor of Mt. Olive Baptist Church in Molena, Georgia. He is married with three wonderful children. His sister Ashley is married with two children, and their mother is enjoying the life of a proud grandmother. They are all doing just fine.

The Very Sad Days of Youth Ministry

Life rarely follows our plans even when you think they are perfect. Sadness and tragedy will affect your youth, but remember, "For you are my hope, o Lord GOD; You are my trust from my youth" (Psalm 71:5). There is a knot that has formed too many times throughout my years in youth ministry. The knots always begin with a phone call. The voice on the other end of the line is usually difficult to understand, and the words seem to come over the line very slowly. It feels like life is rushing around you, but the phone call has stopped time for a brief moment.

It is difficult for me to write this story because as I write I get the familiar knot in the pit of my stomach. On this particular day I was sitting in my favorite ice cream shop in Hendersonville, North Carolina. I had followed my middle school mission team up from Tampa, Florida. They were headed to Asheville with my assistant Luke Eckert. Our youth ministry at Hyde Park UMC was growing, and we were thinking about making Luke the middle school director. He was heading up the mission trip. I was following the group to help them get registered, but I was planning to stay with friends nearby in Spartanburg, South Carolina. I did not expect Luke to need anything because he was truly one of the most capable youth ministers I knew, but I wanted him to feel not only independent but also supported. We had the perfect plan. Little did we know that God had the real perfect plan because he placed each of us in the right place at the right time.

So, there we were eating ice cream and listening to the youth talk about how excited they were about the trip. I was sitting at a table with my friend from South Carolina and one of the senior high helpers named Jena. She came on the middle school mission trip because she was visiting her dad in Texas during the high school trip. Each summer she had been in Texas during both trips, but this year she was able to come back a few days earlier, so she could participate. She was very excited, and I knew she would be an asset to the group. We were all sitting there eating our ice cream and laughing when my phone rang. I answered the phone and the voice on the other line was very quiet, and time stood still. It was the call I was all too familiar with but could never get use to.

As I watched the girl across from me eating her ice cream I knew her life was about to change forever. I knew the smile on her face would soon turn to tears, and her heart would be broken. I closed my phone and just watched her for a few seconds. I wanted her happiness to last every second possible. I needed to plan and get everything in place, so that the staff and I could help Jena to the best of our abilities. I sprang into action. I found Luke, told him what happened, and asked him to find all her luggage and put it in my trunk. I asked my friend to be prepared to drive us back to South Carolina, so I could sit in the back with Jena. Luke's task was to ask Jena to meet me at my car. I would give her the news, and we would head to South Carolina. It was already late in the afternoon, but my husband worked on finding a flight to get her from Spartanburg to Tampa as soon as possible. Luke would prepare the adult leaders then gather the youth to tell them what had happened and pray for Jena and her family.

As Jena approached the car I prayed for her. My prayer consisted of two words, "help her." I asked her to sit beside me in the car. She sat down nervously, closed the door and we were moving. She did not even ask where we were going she just asked "what happened?" There will never be a class or a book that can prepare you for how to tell a teenager their parent has died. You can only ask God for strength and wisdom so you can be the best minister in their time of need.

I wrapped my arms around her and held her the entire trip. When we arrived in Spartanburg we found out the next flight to Tampa was early the next morning. We were staying with my friend Connie who knew too much about grief herself. Her daughter had gone to be with Jesus as a young adult. Connie generously opened her arms and home to Jena. We hugged, cried, prayed and then hugged cried and prayed some more. It was the first time I had ever seen anyone who cried in their sleep. She never stopped. The next morning I flew to Tampa with her and watched her mom and sister embrace her the moment we stepped through security. She was in good hands.

I turned around and flew back to South Carolina. Two hours after I arrived in South Carolina I received a call that another youth needed to be flown home immediately because his brother was in a very serious boating accident and was in intensive care. I drove to the worksite in Asheville, told him what happened, and let him know we had arranged a flight home, so he could be with his family. He asked a lot of questions, and I answered them to the best of my ability. We prayed, hugged, and prayed again. All I could do was remind him that God was with him and he had an entire congregation praying for him and supporting him and his family. His faith was strong and as he entered the plane he told me everything was going to be all right. I guess I looked like I needed reassuring. He wanted to fly alone and I respected his wishes. I think he was stronger than I was at the time. Maybe he knew his brother was a survivor. Maybe God told him through a text message.

I always think of that week as the worse week in the history of youth ministry. The week did not end with flying two youth home. An adult counselor also had to fly home the next day because her father had a heart attack. The week had been so emotional several youth on the trip experienced panic attacks, and one would have ended up in the emergency room if I had not been good friends with a Doctor who offered some great advice and treatment. The adult counselor's father recovered, and Luke stayed in middle school ministry long after this mission trip.

Anger and Hurt Should Not Live Here!

There are times in Youth ministry when you will get angry. I am not talking about the kind of angry you get when the youth roll your house in toilet paper for the thirtieth time, video tape themselves doing it, and send you the tape. I am also not talking about the anger you may have from when your youth put enough furniture for a three bedroom house complete with a stove, refrigerator, sink, toilet, cabinets and beds on your front lawn the day of your wedding as a "wedding gift." I am not even talking about the anger you get when they drop water balloons out the second floor window on the heads of another youth group returning from their Bible study while on a mission trip. No, I am talking about real anger that is so deep that it cannot be expressed in anyway because you are also so filled with sadness that you do not even know you are angry. This has only happened once in twenty years, and it was one too many times.

Adam was a beautiful teenager. He was a blond surfer who loved to have fun. He made me laugh. He was also mischievous. He loved practical jokes, would do anything on a dare, and was famous in our youth group for "mooning." I will not define the word *mooning*. As a youth minister you should know the definition. If not, feel free to "google" the word. I could never stay mad at Adam because he was, well, Adam. No one could stay angry at him for longer than a minute because he would smile, say he was sorry, and that was enough. Adam was an only child. His parents adored him, his friends wanted to be like him, girls wanted to marry him, and strangers wanted to be his friend. It is difficult to believe that Adam is the only youth in all my years of ministry that I have been truly angry with. I am talking about the kind of anger that made me raging mad. I have never felt that toward any youth until the day Adam died. Adam died from a senseless accident. I do not know the details. He was not drinking and driving. It was an accident that could not be explained. No one knows the how or the why. We only know the result. Adam was dead, and it was senseless.

I was asked to speak at Adams funeral by his mother who was and is my good friend. I was filled with mixed emotions. I loved him so much, but when I looked at his mom and dad I was so incredibly angry because he was gone. I was angry at Adam, I was angry at God and I was angry with myself for being angry. I was also immensely sad. I had experienced the loss of a child. I also was now the mother of a blond little boy that reminded me of Adam. How could so much anger and sadness live in my heart? I was a Youth Minister. I needed to be strong for his family, strong for my former youth and strong for his friends. That type of strength can only come from God.

All my feelings were worldly feelings. They were about me and my selfishness. God does not take people from us. He welcomes them home. God had welcomed a beautiful, funny young man home and I needed to focus on what made me love him and what made other people love him. The way a person dies is not a reflection of how they lived. Why was I trying to make that connection? I prayed and began writing the eulogy for Adam's funeral. As I wrote each word the anger began to melt away and peace filled its place. Adam was with God. According to Revelation 3:5 "He is clothed in white garments. " I am sure he has chosen to keep them on.

This chapter was probably not what you expected. Maybe you wanted a schedule of an ordinary day or wondered what the life of a Youth Minister looks like. I guess that was just too difficult for me to write. Youth ministry is about loving youth who do not love themselves and teaching them about a God who loves them unconditionally. He loves them so much that he did something truly outrageous. He sent His son to earth as a helpless baby to be raised by earthly people who are so horrible they chose to kill him in a humiliating way. Then He came back to life and saved them all. Just teach this in an ordinary way, and you will be fine.

Helpful Hint

Youth ministry is about loving youth who do not love themselves and teaching them about a God who loves them unconditionally.

In other words, you have a huge job. You can only do it with the love of Christ, the guidance of the Holy Spirit, and the power of God.

Appendix A

Youth ministry is constantly changing. It is almost impossible to keep up with the culture and trends without networking with other youth ministers and continuing your youth ministry education. Conferences, classes, conventions, and so on will not only renew your spirit for ministry, but will give you the ever-changing tools needed to help you better understand youth, parents, and yourself.

Ask your church if it is willing to make continuing education a part of your salary package so you can provide the best ministry possible. If your church is unable to pay for continuing education, contact organizations or schools and request scholarship information. You may also look for local conventions, training workshops, or classes within your denomination. They are usually budget friendly or free.

Here is a list of some of the best continuing-education opportunities.

Continuing Education

National Youth Workers Convention
> www.youthspecialties.com
> September–October/November—locations vary each year
> Interdenominational

Perkins School of Youth Ministry
> www.smu.edu
> January—Texas
> United Methodist (open to all denominations)

LifeWay National Youth Workers Conference
> http://www.lifeway.com/n/Product
> -Family/LifeWay-National-Youth-Workers
> -Conference?type=events
> September—Nashville, Tennessee
> Southern Baptist (open to all denominations)

Sustainable Youth Ministry Conference
> www.crcna.org
> May—Western Seminary in Holland, Michigan
> Christian Reformed Church in North America
> (open to all denominations)

Center for Youth Ministry Training
> www.cymt.org
> Year-round events—various locations
> Interdenominational

Simply Youth Ministry Conference
> conference.youthministry.com
> March—location varies each year
> Interdenominational

Appendix B

Bibles

- Thomas Nelson, *Revolve Devotional Bible: The Complete Bible for Teen Girls* (Nashville: Thomas Nelson, 2010).
- Thomas Nelson, *Take Action Teen Bible* (Nashville: Thomas Nelson, 2011).

Books

- Jim Burns and Mike DeVries, *Partnering with Parents in Youth Ministry* (Ventura, Calif.: Gospel Light, 2003).
- Jim Burns with Mike DeVries, *Uncommon Youth Ministry: Your Onramp to Launching an Extraordinary Youth Ministry* (Ventura, Calif.: Regal, 2008).
- Chap Clark and Kara E. Powell, *Deep Ministry in a Shallow World: Not-So-Secret Findings about Youth Ministry* (Grand Rapids: Zondervan; El Cajon, Calif.: Youth Specialties, 2006).
- Jessica Tinklenburg DeVega and Christine Ortega Guarkee, *All You Want to Know But Didn't Think You Could Ask: Religions, Cults, and Popular Beliefs* (Nashville: Thomas Nelson, forthcoming).

- Karen Dockrey, *The Youth Worker's Guide to Creative Bible Study,* rev. and exp. ed. (Nashville: Broadman & Holman, 1999).
- Doug Fields, *Purpose Driven Youth Ministry: Nine Essential Foundations for Healthy Growth* (Grand Rapids: Zondervan, 1998).
- Mark Gilroy Communications, *Soul Matters for Teens* (Nashville: J. Countryman, 2005).
- James A. Harnish, *Journey to the Center of the Faith: An Explorer's Guide to Christian Living* (Nashville: Abingdon, 2001).
- Max Lucado and Jenna Lucado Bishop, *You Were Made to Make a Difference* (Nashville: Tommy Nelson, 2010).
- Sean McDowell, ed., *Apologetics for a New Generation: A Biblical and Culturally Relevant Approach to Talking about God* (Eugene, Ore.: Harvest House, 2009).
- Mark Yaconelli, *Contemplative Youth Ministry: Practicing the Presence of Jesus* (Grand Rapids: Zondervan, 2006).

Video Series

- Doug Fields, *The Truth about Sex* (Bluefish TV, 2010).

High Commitment Bible Studies

- *Disciple* (Nashville: Cokesbury).
- *Companions in Christ* (Nashville: Upper Room).
- *The Way of Pilgrimage* (Nashville: Upper Room).